1

More Stars Than Grains of Sand

More Stars than Grains of Sand

Wonders,

Wonderment —

and Religion

Al Forsyth

To Cory and Jenna,
who have so often filled me with wonder and joy

For that's what we humans do as we compare ourselves to others, making spectrums of our experience that inspire with an almost spiritual sense of wonder.
— David Blatner, 2014 [1]

It is enough for me . . . to reflect upon the marvelous structure of the universe and try humbly to comprehend an infinitesimal part of the intelligence manifested in Nature.
— Albert Einstein, 1935 [2]

[1] Blatner, David. *Spectrums: Our Mind-boggling Universe from Infinitesimal to Infinity.* 2012, Bloomsbury: New York. p. 173.

[2] Patrick, George T. W. & Chapman, Frank M. *Introduction to Philosophy.* 1935. Houghton Mifflin: Boston. p. 44.

Table of Contents

FOREWORD

This book is a compendium of facts drawn from scientific research, as reported by others. Many of the facts are cited from secondary or tertiary sources. None represent original research by me.

Among the sources of the facts ("wonders") included here, three stand out, two books by Bill Bryson and one by David Blatner. Bryson's first book, *A Short History of Nearly Everything*, covers, well, nearly everything, in chronicling the advances of scientific knowledge of our world. His second book, *The Body: A Guide for Occupants,* introduces the reader to amazing facts about the amazing human body. Blatner's book, *Spectrums: Our Mind-boggling Universe from Infinitesimal to Infinity,* focuses on scale, on expanding our knowledge and correcting our misconceptions regarding numbers, size, light, sound, heat and time (his chapters). His aim is similar to mine in this book, and there is overlap with my chapters, yet my book has an additional major focus on the living world, on our place as humans within that world. Both Bryson and Blatner express a sense of wonder at the facts they relate, but neither even hints at a relationship between wonder, in the world of science, and religion, as I do. I quote extensively from the two books by Bryson and one by Blatner. I considered paraphrasing their words, but both authors write exquisitely, with clarity, energy and humor – and I strongly recommend that the reader read their works in their entirety.

Blatner, David. *Spectrums: Our Mind-boggling Universe from Infinitesimal to Infinity*. 2012, Bloomsbury: New York.
Bryson, Bill. *A Short History of Nearly Everything*. 2003, Broadway Books (Random House): New York.
_____. *The Body: A Guide for Occupants*. 2019, Doubleday: New York.

INTRODUCTION

WON·der *(verb)* to desire or be curious to know something *(Oxford Languages)*

WON·der *(noun)* a feeling of surprise mingled with admiration, caused by something beautiful, unexpected, unfamiliar, or inexplicable *(Oxford Languages)*

WON·der·ment *(noun)* a state of awed admiration or respect *(Oxford Languages)*

To wonder may lead to revealing wonders, and contemplation of wonders may lead to wonderment.

What are these things I call wonders and why learn about them? Each of the nuggets about the natural world – the world that exists outside of what we humans do or cause – that follows in this book challenges our sense of scale and the boundaries of what we know and are comfortable with in our everyday lives. They expand our existing knowledge in unexpected ways, or introduce information that is new and surprising, or correct past misinformation. In all instances, they were chosen to inspire a sense of wonder, even awe. They are wonder-full and awe-inspiring.

We humans tend to think we are somewhere in the middle on a spectrum of sizes of living things. We can see animals and plants larger than us, with whales and redwood trees at the upper extreme. And we can see animals and plants that are smaller, with tiny flies at our limit of unaided vision. But that's just it: this is what we *see*. We know that there are living things much smaller that we can see with microscopes, like bacteria – but how much smaller? And are there organisms larger than what we see, perhaps below ground? We feel we are "middle-sized" because the limits that we experience with our vision place us there. Seeing is how we experience life every day: we do not spend much time thinking about what is beyond that range of vision.

What do we know about the size of the universe, from our experience? Again, we can *see* the Sun and the Moon and distant stars in the night sky. We know those tiny twinkling stars are farther than the Sun, and the Sun is farther than the Moon. But how far? Are the stars a hundred times as far as the Sun? A thousand? More? And are all those stars pretty much equally distant from us? And how large are they? We are a speck in a vast universe, but how vast is it and how speck-like are we? We are told that such smallness should make us feel humble or grateful to be alive or some such, and we may actually feel that. But unless we know what is out there – how big and how far – can we have a proper sense of our place?

What about numbers of things? There are almost eight billion human beings on Earth, and counting. Is that a lot? How does that compare with numbers of other organisms? Are we "in the middle"? It may feel so: we don't see many elephants or rabbits or even fish. And at the other end of the numbers curve, we know there are a lot more microbes than us. But how many? Without knowledge, we may feel "middling" simply by default. With knowledge, we may find that we are mistaken.

How about kinds of other living things? We are just one species, *Homo sapiens*, and we know of course that there are more species of other kinds of animals and plants. But is it five times as many? A hundred times? A thousand? Still more? Intuitively, we may feel that the more species of a kind of animal, the more successful that animal is, in evolutionary terms. Or is it the opposite?

One area where we "know" we humans excel all other species is intelligence – our human exceptionalism. But are we really so sure of that? Just what *is* intelligence? And does it matter that we humans are the ones doing the defining and measuring?

Beyond intelligence, how do we stack up with the rest of the living world on other traits? Take the senses: we know we do not have the best eyesight or hearing or taste or smell, but are we in the middle of some range on these? How far are we from the very best? And what about other traits, like speed and strength, not to mention less easily measurable traits such as durability, resilience and the like? Just where do we humans stand?

What we know is that which we experience and that which we accept of what others tell us. Science adds to our knowledge, expands our horizons, but mostly we do not seek out the enlightenment that science offers. Our lives are full enough; our attention is focused on the day-to-day. We have to make an effort to explore new boundaries, to place ourselves ever more accurately in the grand scheme of things. Is it worth the effort? I gently argue in this book that it is. I contend that the journey of expanding our boundaries through contemplating these new revelations of knowledge, these wonders, and of re-thinking the scale of things and where on the various spectrums we exist, leads to wonderment.

How small is small? How large is large? How far is far? How much is a whole lot? How old is old? How special are our human abilities? It is these questions that the wonders in this book touch upon. Science can provide answers – some very exact, some less so – to these questions. If we accept these answers, if we expand and deepen our understanding of the natural world and where we are in it, I contend we will arrive, in possibly a religious sense, at wonderment, at awe.

NOTES TO THE READER

This is a book to be read slowly. Fifty-two wonders are presented, not coincidentally the same number as weeks in the year. While reading each wonder will take at most a few minutes, try to absorb it slowly and let it percolate. Take a couple of days at least, and preferably a week, to let these facts bang around in your brain and leave an impression. Ask yourself the following questions before moving on:

• What did I just learn?

• What did it mean?

• How does it make me feel differently about the world?

• How does it make me feel differently about myself in the world?

Reading this book, you may feel overwhelmed by an avalanche of numbers. This is another reason to take each wonder slowly. Specific numbers are given, but the important thing is to recognize and understand the magnitude of the numbers, not learn their precise values – average; large; very large; very, very large; almost unfathomably large; small; really small; really, really small; almost infinitesimally small, etc. An introductory section on understanding large and small numbers may help in this effort.

This book is a compendium of facts, but it is also a compendium of _opinions_ and _"best guesses"_, taken from different, reputable sources. For many of the questions addressed in this book, there is not one, single, universally-agreed-upon answer, but a range of scientifically-arrived-at best guesses. Such is the nature of science and the quest for knowledge. For example, how many species are there on Earth – 8.7 million? 10 million? 14 million? One hundred million?! Something else? You will encounter what appear to be disagreements among scientists. There are many fields of inquiry introduced in this book where research is just beginning and where precision and agreement are far down the road. Try not to become frustrated by this imprecision. Try not to get bogged down in trying to determine "right answers": instead, try to ascertain the "general truth" or trend behind the range of opinions. In the case of the number of species, if you come away recognizing that there is a very large number of species, in the millions, and we have documented or described only a small percentage of them – facts on which all scientists agree – that is enough to awaken wonder.

To wonder is to unleash our curiosity and ask why or how. The answers may be wonders like those in this book. And those wonders may lead to wonderment. Let the journey begin. But first . . .

UNDERSTANDING NUMBERS LARGE AND SMALL

Our experience with numbers is usually quite limited. We deal typically in a handful of fractions, single digits, tens, hundreds, but not much beyond that. Sports arenas and stadiums hold tens of thousands of spectators, so if we attend those events we may understand such numbers. We may live in communities of hundreds of thousands of people, or even millions, but the numbers are abstract – we never *see* that many people all at once. Beyond millions, we hear numbers such as billions and even trillions usually in terms of money amounts – budgets, deficits, government expenditures, Gross National Products – but do we really have a grasp of the magnitude of such numbers? They are more than the tens, hundreds and thousands that we may experience directly, but how much more?

This introductory section provides bases in reality for large (and small) numbers by relating them to familiar objects that we can visualize, or actions that we are familiar with. What size spaces would a million, a billion or a trillion goldfish occupy? How long would it take to count to one million, one billion or one trillion? The answers will surprise. Once we can grasp how large millions and billions and trillions – and even larger numbers – are, we have a better understanding of *small* numbers as well – millionths, billionths, trillionths and even smaller.

We may cross paths infrequently, if at all, with very large and very small numbers in our daily lives, but when we explore wonders of the natural world, they are crucial to our understanding and to our appreciation of their very wonder. In fact, those numbers may elevate a merely interesting fact to a true, jaw-dropping wonder. Very large and very small numbers may transform a sense of wonder into a state of true wonderment.

A note on scientific notation:
Very large or small numbers are often cumbersome to write, especially if they are beyond trillions and trillionths. Certainly writing them out in words is cumbersome, but even writing them as ordinary numbers is awkward. Consider 28,009,454,330,786: that's the US national debt in dollars at this writing, or twenty-eight trillion nine billion four hundred fifty-four million three hundred thirty thousand seven hundred eighty-six dollars. Whew, too much to handle. And even the names for very large numbers are not always enlightening:
a thousand trillions is a quadrillion;
a thousand quadrillions is a quintillion;
a thousand quintillions is a sextillion;
a thousand sextillions is a septillion;
a thousand septillions is an octillion;
a thousand octillions is a nonillion;

a thousand nonillions is a decillion;
and on and on, *ad* (almost) *infinitum*.

Scientific notation is a shortcut to writing very large and small numbers so that they are more easily understandable. Any number can be written as some number times a power of 10.
So, $34 = 3.4 \times 10^1$ or 3.4 times 10;
and $3.4 = 3.4 \times 10^0$ or 3.4 times 1;
and $340 = 3.4 \times 10^2$ or 3.4 x 10x 10, or 100;
and $3,400 = 3.4 \times 10^3$ or 3.4 x 10 x 10 x 10, or 1,000;
etc.
Because $10^3 = 1,000$, then $10^6 = 10^3 \times 10^3 = 1,000 \times 1,000$ or 1 million (1,000,000);
and $10^9 = 1$ million x 1,000 or 1 billion (1,000,000,000);
and $10^{12} = 1$ billion x 1,000 or 1 trillion (1,000,000,000,000).
Each time you multiply by 1,000, you add three more zeroes before the decimal point and jump to the next big number word.
For example, $10^{18} = 1$ trillion (10^{12}) x 1,000 x 1,000 or 1 followed by 18 zeroes (or 1 quintillion).

Scientific notation for very small numbers turns very large numbers into fractions, by putting a negative sign before the exponent.
So $10^{-2} = 1/10^2$ or 1/100 or 1 one-hundredth;
and $3.4 \times 10^{-2} = 3.4 \times 1/100$ or 3.4 one-hundredths.

It's all a lot to hold in one's head, but it will become easier to grasp as you confront more and more large and small numbers in the wonders that follow in this book. Referring back to this introduction as you encounter such numbers may be helpful.

Note: To help appreciate the magnitude of a million, a billion and a trillion below, I have included several analogies, several ways of looking at and thinking about those numbers, not just one. My goal is to find one or more that work particularly well for you, and we will all have different preferences. The same applies later, in the wonders themselves.

THE WONDERS

NUMBERS

WONDER 1 – How Much is a Million?

This first wonder is kind of a practice one. The information may not be as enlightening as that which is to follow. And yet, try to absorb it slowly and let it brew. This wonder will provide a baseline with regard to your understanding of quantity, which is behind so many wonders. Think about the following examples and analogies as you encounter large numbers in your daily life and in the media – and see if they don't have new meaning.

A million is 1,000,000, or a thousand thousands. So how big is a thousand. Well, one thousand seconds equals 16 minutes 40 seconds.
And counting from one to one thousand as fast as you can would take you about 10 minutes.

Now, how big is a million?
One million seconds equals 277 hours 50 minutes, or 11.57 days.
Counting from one to one million would take you 23 days nonstop, at an ambitious counting rate of two seconds per number. [1]

A human tower of one million kids (average height 4'8" (1.45 m)) standing on each other's shoulders would be 4 million feet (1,219,200 m) high or 757.5 miles (1,219 km) high. [1]

A goldfish bowl big enough for 1 million goldfish would be big enough for a whale. [1]

If you earned $1 per second ($3,600 per hour), you'd have $1 million in 11.6 days.

Now take a look at the opposite page. It shows 10,000 dots. It would take a book with 100 pages like that to contain 1 million dots.

Sources:
[1] Schwartz, David M. *How Much Is a Million?* 1985, Lothrop, Lee & Shepard Books (William Morrow & Company): New York. (unpaginated)

WONDER 2 – How Much is a Billion?

Now we start to get into territory unfamiliar to most of us. We hear about billions of people in the world or billions of dollars spent or an extremely wealthy person's billions, but what does that mean? How big are those numbers *really*.

A billion is 1,000,000,000, or one thousand million (and, again, one million is a thousand thousand).
One billion seconds equals 11,574 days, or 31.69 years – quite a jump from the 11.57 days that equal one *million* seconds.
Counting from one to one billion would take you 95 years nonstop, many years more than an average lifetime, at a counting rate of rate of 3 seconds per number. (That counting rate is likely way too fast when you are counting aloud numbers like 787,597,657 or "seven hundred eighty-seven million five hundred ninety-seven thousand six hundred fifty-seven".) [1]

A human tower of one billion kids would be higher than the distance from Earth to the Moon, which is 238,900 miles (384,472 km)! [1]

Remember the whale-size goldfish bowl that could contain one million goldfish? Well, it would take a thousand of those giant goldfish bowls, or a goldfish bowl the size of a football stadium to hold one *billion* goldfish. [1]

If you earned $1 per second ($3,600 per hour), you'd have $1 billion in 31.7 years.

"To visualize a billionth of anything, consider half the width of your little fingernail compared with the distance from New York to Los Angeles." [2]

Before ending this wonder, go back to the page with the 10,000 dots. A book with 100 such pages would contain 1 million dots. And it would take 1 thousand such books to hold 1 *billion* dots.

Sources:
[1] *How Much . . . .*
[2] Blatner, David. *Spectrums: Our Mind-boggling Universe from Infinitesimal to Infinity.* 2012, Bloomsbury: New York, p. 47.
Photo: University of Georgia football stadium (MaxPixel -- Google Creative Commons)

WONDER 3 – How Much is a Trillion?

Ready for a quantum leap? We increasingly hear about billions – number of humans on Earth, wealth of our wealthiest people, expenditures of governments – but trillions are less common in daily parlance. It is creeping into the world of finance of wealthy countries (for example, the US National Debt is in the tens of trillions of dollars). When we hear "trillions", we react kind of as we do to "billions" – it's just another very large amount. However, the size of the leap from billions to trillions may surprise you. A trillion is a very, *very* large amount!

A trillion is 1,000,000,000,000, or a thousand billion (and one billion is a thousand million).
One trillion seconds equals 31,688 years!
The US has not existed for a trillion seconds. In fact, Western civilization has not been around a trillion seconds. In fact, one trillion seconds ago Neanderthals inhabited the plains of Europe.

How long would it take to count from one to one trillion (1,000,000,000,000)? At one number per second, 31,688 years. But realistically, because numbers become more polysyllabic the higher you go, the average time to say each number might be six seconds, so it would take 190,259 years! [1]

A human tower of one trillion kids would stretch from Earth to Saturn's rings when that planet is at its closest to Earth, or 734 million miles (1.17 billion km). [1]

A stack of $1 bills equal to $1 trillion would be 70,000 miles high.

One trillion goldfish would completely fill a big city harbor, or a thousand football stadiums. [1]

If you earned $1 per second ($3,600 per hour), you'd have $1 trillion in 31,688 years.

Back to the page with 10,000 dots, and the book with 100 pages (1 million dots), and the 1 thousand such books (1 billion dots), it would take 1 million such books of 1,000 pages each to total 1 trillion dots.

Sources:
[1] *How Much* . . . .
Photo: New York City harbor (Wikimedia Commons – Google Creative Commons)

WONDER 4 – Million vs. Billion vs. Trillion

A million seconds is 12 days.
A billion seconds is 31 years.
A trillion seconds is 31,688 years.

A million minutes ago was 1 year, 329 days, 10 hours, 40 minutes ago.
A billion minutes ago was just after the time of Christ.
A trillion minutes ago was 1,901,280 years ago.

A million hours ago was in 1885.
A billion hours ago man had not yet walked on Earth.
A trillion hours ago was more than 114 million years ago, the age of
Tyrannosaurus Rex (the Cretaceous Period).

Let's take one more look at millions, billions and trillions, in terms of metric distance.
One millimeter is about the thickness of a dime.
Walking a million millimeters (1,000 meters) would take less than an hour.
Driving a billion millimeters (1 million meters or 625 miles) would take 10 hours.
A trillion millimeters is equal to 25 times around Earth. Or, back to the dimes one millimeter thick, a stack of a trillion dimes would circle Earth 25 times.

To get a better feel for the magnitude of differences among thousands, millions, billions and trillions, take a look at the US "debt clock":
https://www.usdebtclock.org
The numbers are changing incredibly rapidly. The smaller numbers – single digits (impossible to see), tens (ditto), hundreds (ditto), thousands (ditto), tens of thousands (barely visible), hundreds of thousands (finally slow enough to count) – change very rapidly, but the millions, tens of millions and hundreds of millions change much more slowly. You will have to wait quite a while to see

the billions change. Don't think of waiting wait around for the trillions. And then look back at the single digits flying by. Trillions are huge numbers!

Here are two good websites for calculating large numbers that could be handy if you want to delve further into some of the numerical wonders that follow:
https://www.dcode.fr/big-numbers-division
https://www.dcode.fr/big-numbers-multiplication

Sources:
[1] *Spectrums,* p. 18.
Photo: *Tyrannosaurus Rex* (Pxfuel – Google Creative Commons)

WONDER 5 – Other Very Large Numbers

Beyond a trillion:

1 thousand trillion = 1 quadrillion (15 zeroes) = 1,000,000,000,000,000
$= 10^{15}$

1 million trillion = 1 quintillion (18 zeroes) =
1,000,000,000,000,000,000 = 10^{18}

1 billion trillion = 1 sextillion (21 zeroes) =
1,000,000,000,000,000,000,000 = 10^{21}

And so on.

If you counted by millions and added 1 million each second, it would take more than 30 million years to reach a sextillion!

The doubling phenomenon:

If you place one grain of rice on the first square of a chessboard, then two on the next square, then four on the next, then 8, then 16, etc., by the time you place the last pile on the 64th square, there will be enough grains of rice on the board "to fill a box 4 miles (6.43 km) long, 4 miles (6.4 km) wide, and 6 miles (9.6 km) high – taller than Mt. Everest." (That's 1.84×10^{19} grains of rice!) [1]

What is a "googol"?

A googol equals 10^{100} = 10 x 10 x 10 . . . one hundred times or 10 followed by 100 zeroes. This is more than the number of molecules in every substance on Earth and more than all the hydrogen atoms that make up the Sun.

In fact, *every atom in the known universe* = 10^{81} = a quintillion *less* than a googol. [2]

An even larger number, truly ridiculously large, is a "googolplex", equal to 10^{googol} or 10 x 10 x 10 . . . googol times.

Very large numbers come into play when talking about the speed of light and light-years.

Nothing travels faster than light. It travels through the vacuum of space at 186,000 miles/second (300,000 km/sec).

One light-year is the distance light travels through space in one year, which is 5.9 trillion miles (9.44 trillion km).

Light from the Sun takes 8 minutes 20 seconds to reach Earth, covering 93,000,000 miles (150,000,000 km) in the process. You could say that the Sun is 8 1/3 *light-minutes* from Earth.

So, a light-year sounds like a measure of time, but it's really a measure of distance – extreme distance.

An aside on the speed of light: it could travel 7.5 times around Earth in a single second. The Moon is just over one light-second from Earth.

If light leaves the Sun at 12:00am January 1, at 12:08 it reaches Earth; at 1:00am it passes Jupiter (1 light-hour away); at midnight (1 light-day), it passes the Kuiper Belt, a visible disc of stars in the outer solar system; in 27 days, it reaches the Oort Cloud, a predicted but not yet observed collection of ice objects in the cold recesses of the solar system. And that's just our solar system, part of the Milky Way galaxy, one of innumerable galaxies in the universe. [3]

More on light-years of distance in the next section of this book.

Sources:
[1] *Spectrums*, p. 14.
[2] *Spectrums*, p. 20.
[3] *Spectrums*, p. 39-40.
Photo: Chessboard with piles of rice (Flickr/Audrey Penven – Google Creative Common)

THE NON-LIVING WORLD

Scale: The Very, Very Large

Look up, into the night sky. With insignificant shifts in star position and some changes in total numbers, you are seeing the exact same thing that the very first human eyes saw, more than 300,000 years ago. And it is roughly the same celestial scene that our first primate ancestor's eyes saw, more than 50 *million* years ago. The same pricks of white-silver light, some shimmering; the same milky ribbon of gauze; the same dark void.

The earliest eyes we know about would have seen no further than the same inconceivably far-off boundary of the known that we see. It is, and has always been, the upper end of the scale of distance with the naked eye. But today we have telescopes to extend our sight and radio telescopes to detect radio waves given off by objects incredibly far off in space.

What did the first human think when he looked skyward? No doubt different thoughts than our gaze inspires today. We know so much more about things distant. What do *you* think looking into that night sky? What will you think after reading on?

The wonders in this section will challenge your understanding of scale, of how big the universe is and of how large and small the objects within it are. This is mostly macro scale stuff – in fact, it doesn't get more macro in terms of spatial dimensions. The universe is very, very big. And very, very empty. And yet contains a very, very large number of stars and planets. The sizes of stars and planets cover an immense range. Some objects are much bigger than we might think; some are relatively much smaller.

Our visual representation of our solar system is typically a classroom mobile of the Sun and nine planets (or eight since Pluto's demotion to a dwarf planet in 2006). In this section, you will discover just how misleading such a representation is. As for the rest of our galaxy and the universe, we just do not have any good representations. The wonders in this section will provide some.

WONDER 6 – The Outer Edge of What We Know

How do we form our conception of the universe? We look into the night sky and see stars – but it turns out we see only a small fraction of them and only the nearest ones. We see photos or drawings of the Milky Way, the galaxy (system of stars and planets) of which our Sun and our solar system of planets are a part – but there are *billions* of galaxies, and our solar system is only a tiny part of the Milky Way galaxy. We may remember the solar system mobile hanging in a classroom and conclude that it comprises most of the universe – but of course it is only an infinitesimal part and the relative sizes of the Sun and planets in the mobile, and the distances between them, are way off. So our conception is flawed, warped and incomplete.

What is the correct conception of the universe and our place in it? How far off is our misconception?

The farthest known thing in the universe is 10 trillion times farther from Earth than the Sun is.

Where is the ultimate boundary, the edge of the universe? Simply put, we don't know. But we do know that it's beyond the farthest thing we have *measured*, which is galaxy GN-z11, discovered in 2016 by the Hubble space telescope. ("GN" refers to the "galaxy name" and "z11" refers to its brightness.) It is 13.4 billion light-years away, so the light that enables us to see this galaxy was emitted 8.9 billion years before Earth was formed (4.5 billion years ago), and just 400 million years after the universe was born (or less than 3% of the way into its life to date). One light-year is equal to 5.9 trillion miles (9.44 trillion km), so GN-z11 is at least 5.9 trillion x 13.4 billion miles away, or 79×10^{21}, or 79 with 21 zeroes after it, or 79 sextillion miles (126 sextillion km) away. By contrast, the Sun is 93 million miles (150 million km) from Earth, or about one ten-trillionth (1×10^{-13}) of the distance to GN-z11. The light from the Sun takes "only" a little over 8 minutes to reach Earth. [1]

We are truly a speck in space.

The farthest thing we can see is less than one one-thousandth of the way to the farthest known thing, and the farthest discrete object is one-millionth of the way there.

The farthest we can see in the sky with the naked eye, on a really dark night, is the fuzzy center of the Andromeda galaxy, 2.5 million light-years away, or 14.7×10^{18} or 14.7 quintillion miles (23.5 quintillion km) from Earth. That's a very long way, but it's less than one one-thousandth of the way to the farthest known thing in the universe, galaxy GN-z11.

The farthest *discrete object* we can see with the naked eye is the star V762 Cas, a star in the Cassiopeia galaxy, which is 16,308 light-years away. That's about 96×10^{15} or 96 quadrillion miles (153.6 quadrillion km) from Earth. Again, a very long way, but only about one-thousandth of the way to the Andromeda galaxy, and only one-millionth of the way to the farthest known thing, galaxy GN-z11. [2]

Sources:
[1] Independent: "Most distant object in the universe spotted by Hubble Space Telescope, shattering record for the farthest known galaxy"   https://bit.ly/3tiJopH
[2] Quora.com: "Which is the farthest object from Earth visible to the naked eye?" https://bit.ly/32hUqPY
Photo: Milky Way (Public Domain Pictures – Google Creative Commons) [caption added]

WONDER 7 – The Enormity of Space

The universe is joltingly huge and is mostly just empty space.

Vast numbers of stars and galaxies fill the universe, but what really fills it is empty space. It is so immense that it can swallow up prodigious numbers of celestial bodies and still seem very, very empty.
Close to home, space is enormous, but nothing like it is farther away.
The Moon is about 250,000 miles (384,000 km) from Earth, or 10 times the circumference of Earth. The closest planet to us (Venus) is about 25 million miles (40 million km) away –100 times the distance between the Moon and Earth. [1]

If the solar system were the size of a classroom, the Sun floating in middle would be the size of grain of salt; and Earth would be the size of a bacterium 10 cm (4 in) away. Or if the Earth were the size of a grain of salt, the solar system out to Neptune would be 352 m (1,154 ft) wide – 3.5 football fields of mostly empty space. Out to the Oort Cloud (virtually the whole solar system) would be more than 2,000 times more space; a grain of salt in an area 450 miles (724 km) wide. [2]

The Sun is a star, the center of our solar system. The nearest star to our Sun is Proxima Centauri, 4.3 light-years away, a hundred million times further than the Moon. "To reach it by spaceship would take at least twenty-five thousand years . . . . Just reaching the center of our own galaxy would take far longer than we have existed as beings." [3]

If our Sun were the size of a grapefruit in Los Angeles, then Alpha Centauri A (a star near Proxima Centauri in a small cluster of stars) would be another, slightly larger grapefruit in Chicago. "If we could send a rocket toward [Alpha Centauri A] at 50,000mph (80,000 km/h), it would take 57,000 years to arrive." [4]

There are about 100 billion stars ("suns") in the Milky Way galaxy of which our solar system is a tiny part. Yet the *average* distance between stars is about 30 trillion miles (48 trillion km). [5]

"If we could build a spaceship that traveled at the speed of light, a million years wouldn't get us to even the halfway point on a journey to the Andromeda galaxy", the farthest thing we can see with the naked eye, 2.5 million light-years away. [6]

There is a *lot* of space in space!

All of the "stuff" in our solar system – Sun, planets and their moons, billions of asteroids and comets – fills less than one-trillionth of the space available in the solar system. And if you traveled from the Sun to Pluto, you would be only one fifty-thousandth of the way to the solar system's edge (at the far edge of the Oort Cloud of drifting comets). [7]

How big is our solar system in relation to our galaxy, the Milky Way? If the solar system (out to Pluto) were shrunk to the size of a quarter, our galaxy would be as big as the western half of the US. [8]

If the Sun were reduced to the size of a soccer ball, Pluto would be 10 football fields away and smaller than a pinhead, and the nearest star would be 4200 miles away.

If the Sun were reduced to the size of a soccer ball, the closest planet, Mercury, would be 10 paces away and the size of a pinhead; Venus would be another 9 paces away and the size of a BB; Earth would be 7 more paces away (26 paces total from the Sun) and also about the size of a BB; Mars would be 14 more paces away and the size of a pinhead; Jupiter would be 95 more paces away and the size of a bottle cap; Saturn would be another 112 paces away and the size of a marble; Uranus would be another 249 paces away and the size of a kernel of corn; Neptune would be 281 more paces and the size of another corn kernel; and Pluto would be 242 more paces and smaller than a pinhead. In this model, at this scale, you would not be able to see any planet from the Sun (because they would be so small). The total distance from the soccer ball Sun to the pinhead Pluto would be about 1,000 yards (914 m), or 10 football fields. And the nearest star, Proxima Centauri, would be 4,200 *miles* (6760 km) away! [9]

There is *really* a lot of space in space!

Not even close to scale

Sources:

[1] *Spectrums*, p. 35.

[2] *Spectrums*, p. 37.

[3] Bryson, Bill. *A Short History of Nearly Everything*. 2003, Broadway Books (Random House): New York, p. 48.

[4] *Spectrums*, p. 40.

[5] Quora.com: "What is the average distance between stars throughout the galaxy and does the mean distance decrease towards the center of the galaxy?"   https://bit.ly/2QD4AYR

[6] *Spectrums*, p. 147.

[7] *A Short History . . .*, p. 25.

[8] *Spectrums*, p. 41.

[9] Cassidy, John. *Earthsearch: A Kid's Geography Museum in a Book*. 1994, Klutz Press: Palo Alto, CA, pp. 59-61.

Photo: Solar System Model (Flickr – Google Creative Commons) [caption added]

WONDER 8 – Sizes of Objects in the Universe

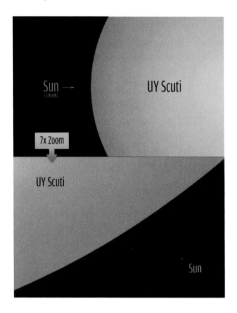

The largest star we can see with the naked eye is one billion times larger than the Sun.

The Sun is the largest object in our solar system, with a diameter of about 836,000 miles (1,338,000 km). You could fit 1.3 million Earths (diameter = 7,600 miles/12,160 km) inside the Sun. The Sun is 23.3 million times larger than Mercury, our smallest planet, and 988 times larger than Jupiter, our largest planet. [1]

However, the Sun is a small star. The largest star we can see with our naked eye is Mu Cephei, in the constellation Cepheus. It is 100,000 times brighter than the Sun and one *billion* times larger. One billion Suns would fit in the volume of Mu Cephei. And 1.3 quadrillion (1.3 x 10^{15}) Earths would fit inside it. And the largest known object in the universe, the star named UY Scuti, is almost twice as large as Mu Cephei! [2]

Note: The relative sizes of planets in our solar system and stars in the universe are shown very dramatically by the following short YouTube video: Planets' and stars' size comparison: https://bit.ly/2Sk1j1F

So cosmically speaking, Earth is very small. How small? Consider the formation of our solar system and of Earth.

"About 4.6 billion years ago, a great swirl of gas and dust some 15 billion miles (24 billion km) across accumulated in space. Virtually all of it – 99.9% of the mass of the solar system – went to make the Sun. Out of the floating material that was left over, two microscopic grains floated close enough together to be joined by electrostatic forces. This was the moment of conception for our planet." [3]

If the Sun is 99.9% of the mass of the solar system, then Jupiter, the largest planet, is a big part of the remaining 0.1%. Jupiter is more than twice the mass of all the other seven planets put together. [4]

If Earth were shrunk to the size of a billiard ball, it would be smoother than the billiard ball.

Comparison with some other planets and with stars shows that Earth is small, a speck in space. But to us, standing on its surface, it seems immense. If it were possible to walk around the circumference of Earth at the equator, it would be a journey of almost 25,000 miles (40,000 km). Walking 20 miles (32 km) a day, it would take 1,250 days, or almost three and a half years.

At its surface, Earth seems anything but smooth, with mountains and valleys everywhere on the land. Yet, if the world were shrunk down to the size of a billiard ball, it would be smoother than a billiard ball! [5]

And "If Earth were shrunk to the size of a wet tennis ball, our atmosphere would be no thicker than the water clinging to the surface." [6]

So, depending on the scale of reference, Earth is either very small or very large.

Sources:

[1] Astronoo.com: "Comparative sizes of planets and stars"   https://bit.ly/3mWbViB

[2] Quora.com: "What is the largest star visible with the naked eye? How big is it?"
https://bit.ly/3earu29

[3] *A Short History . . .*, p. 38.

[4] *Spectrums*, p. 36.

[5] curioser.co.uk: "Proof that the Earth is smoother than a billiard ball"   https://bit.ly/3gjRDy4

[6] *Spectrums*, p. 33.

Photos: Sun and Y Scuti star (Wikimedia Commons – Google Creative Commons); Earth (Flickr – Google Creative Commons); billiard ball (Pixabay – Google Creative Commons)

WONDER 9 – Numbers in the Universe: Stars and Galaxies

There are one billion trillion stars, but only six thousand are visible to the naked eye, or six quadrillionths of the total.

We've seen that there is a lot of space in space: just the distances between planets in our solar system is enormous compared to the size of the planets and the Sun. Yet, there are many, many stars, plus countless planets in the universe.

"Only about six thousand stars are visible to the naked eye from Earth, and only about two thousand can be seen from any one spot. With binoculars, the number . . . rises to about fifty thousand, and with a small 2-inch telescope it leaps to three hundred thousand." [1]

But we are seeing an incredibly small part of the whole. The estimated total number of stars in the observable universe? One billion trillion (1,000,000,000,000,000,000,000) or 1 x 10^{21} or one sextillion. [2]

If galaxies were frozen peas, there would be enough to fill a professional basketball arena.

There is a huge number of stars in the universe, so it's no surprise that there is a huge number of galaxies, or swirling systems of stars grouped together by gravity.
Using the Hubble telescope, astronomers believe there are almost 150 billion galaxies in the visible universe. That's entire galaxies, like the Milky Way which contains about 200 billion stars and 100 billion planets. [3]

"If galaxies were frozen peas, it would be enough to fill a large auditorium – the old Boston Garden, say, or the Royal Albert Hall." [4]

There are millions of galaxies in the "bowl" of the Big Dipper. The lights of whole galaxies blend together to form pinpoints of "stars" that we see. [5]

Given these mind-boggling numbers of stars and galaxies, it is no wonder scientists believe there is very probably (most think almost certainly) life as we know it elsewhere in the universe.

There are more stars in the universe than grains of sand on all Earth's beaches.

Think of sand. Think of tiny grains of sand on a beach. Think of *all* the grains of sand on *all* the beaches on Earth.

And now think of all the stars in the sky, in the universe.

Are there more stars in the universe or grains of sand on all the beaches on Earth?

An estimate of the number of stars in the universe is between 10 sextillion (10^{22}) and 200 sextillion. An estimate of the number of grains of sand on Earth's beaches is 2.5 sextillion to 10 sextillion. So, most probably, there are 5 to 10 times more stars than grains of sand. Something to contemplate next time you are at a beach or gazing at the night sky. [2]

Sources:
[1] *A Short History . . .*, p. 33.
[2] UCSB Scienceline: "About how many stars are in space?"   https://bit.ly/2Q5GIxu
[3] *Spectrums*, p. 18.
[4] *A Short History . . .*, p. 129.
[5] *Spectrums*, p. 44
Photos: Boston Garden (Flickr/Rene Schwietzke – Google Creative Commons); Stars and beach (Piqsels – Google Creative Commons)

WONDER 10 – Water on Earth

The water in Earth's oceans would fill more than 352 quintillion gallon-size milk containers.

Many humans never see an ocean, so they – and even the rest of us who have – might find it hard to believe that more than 97% of the water on Earth is in the oceans. The average depth of the world's oceans is about 12,100 feet (3,688 m), which means that the oceans contain 321,003,271 cubic miles of water. (For comparison, Mt. Everest, Earth's tallest mountain, has a volume of about 14.3 cubic miles.) This equates to 352,670,000,000,000,000,000 or 352.67 quintillion gallons. It takes about 1,050,000,000 (1.05 billion) gallons of water to fill a large football stadium (Dallas Cowboys Stadium, for example), so the world's oceans contain about 336 billion football stadiums of water. [1]

Of the total water on Earth, 97% is salt water in the oceans (or more accurately "world ocean" because all oceans are connected); 3% is fresh water. Of the 3% that is fresh water, only 1.2% is liquid water on the surface. Of that small amount, only 20% is in lakes. So only 0.0072% (or 72-hundred-thousandths percent) of Earth's water is in lakes. And rivers contain only about one-fortieth as much water as lakes. So if the liquid water that most of us see is in rivers and lakes, no wonder our conception of the quantity of water on Earth is flawed. [2]

Side note: More than half the oxygen we breathe comes from ocean plants – photosynthesizers like phytoplankton, seaweed and algae. So "Thank you, ocean." [3]

Sources:
[1] National Ocean Service: "How much water is in the ocean?"   https://bit.ly/3dtJTr
National Ocean Service: "How deep is the ocean?"   https://bit.ly/3syE93P
weightofstuff.com: "How much does Mt. Everest weigh?"   https://bit.ly/3v098rs

prezi.com: "How much water would it take to fill?"   https://bit.ly/3suYxms
[2] USGS.gov: "Where is Earth's water?"   https://on.doi.gov/3duXNcS
[3] Smithsonian (ocean.si.edu): "With every breath you take, thank the ocean"
https://s.si.edu/32rLTKG
Photo: Dallas Cowboys Stadium (Wikimedia Commons – Google Creative Commons) [caption added]

Scale: The Very, Very Small

The past few pages have zoomed out from human scale to the very, very large – in fact, to the largest that we know. Now it's time to jolt our perception again by zooming in to the very, very small.

We may come to this section familiar with some models of very, very small things like molecules and atoms. We will see how inadequate they are. Atoms and their components are far smaller than most of us realize, and therefore incredibly numerous. Just as the world of the very large stretches far beyond the fuzzy star that is the most distant we can see with the naked eye, so the very small is far, far tinier than the speck of dust that is the smallest object our unaided eye can see. This section and the first section will complete the spectrum of spatial dimensions of the universe we inhabit.

WONDER 11 -- Atoms

An average atom is 1/500,000 of the width of a human hair.

What's the smallest thing we can see with our naked eye? A speck of dust? The width of a human hair, about 0.04 millimeters wide? [1]
 "Half a million atoms lined up shoulder to shoulder could hide behind a human hair." [2]

This hyphen (-) is one millimeter long. An atom is one ten-millionth of a millimeter. One atom is to one millimeter "as the thickness of a sheet of paper is to the height of the Empire State Building." [3]

Atoms are tiny!

If you wanted to see an atom in a drop of water, you'd have to enlarge the drop to 14 miles across.

Divide this hyphen (-) into 1,000 equal widths: each is a micron. A paramecium is 2 microns wide. "If you wanted to see with your naked eye a paramecium swimming in a drop of water, you would have to enlarge the drop until it was some 39 feet (12 m) across. However, if you wanted to see the *atoms* in the same drop, you would have to make the drop 14 *miles* (22.4 km) across. [4]

"The ink that forms a single letter 'A' on this page contains enough atoms so that not only could every person on Earth have one, but also every person on every planet in the Milky Way, assuming every star had a planet like ours." (Again, there are about 100 billion planets in the Milky Way.) [5]

Atoms are *really* tiny!

Sources:
[1] Science focus: "How small can the naked eye see?"   https://bit.ly/3edn7TV
[2] *A Short History* . . ., p. 134.
[3] *A Short History* . . ., p. 135.
[4] *A Short History* . . ., p. 134.
[5] *Spectrums*, p. 48.
Photo: Woman with black hair (Piqsels – Google Creative Commons)

WONDER 12 – Parts of an Atom

Just like outer space, so inner space, inside an atom, is mostly empty. But what's there, the parts of the atoms, are amazing.

The nucleus of an atom is very tiny, but very heavy.

Looking at the drawing of the parts of an atom, we might assume that the nucleus at the center occupies a great deal of the atom's space. Not so. "The size of a hydrogen atom . . . Is about 50,000 times larger than the nucleus itself." [1]

"The nucleus of an atom is tiny – only one-millionth of a billionth [one quadrillionth or 1×10^{-15}] of the full volume of the atom – but . . . it contains virtually all of the atom's mass . . . . If an atom were expanded to the size of a cathedral, the nucleus would be only about the size of a fly – but a fly many thousands of times heavier than the cathedral." [2]

Electrons are even tinier than nuclei – and behave very strangely.

"Within every atom [of every chemical element] there is a central nucleus, which contains protons and neutrons, surrounded by varying numbers of electrons [from 1 to 118, depending on the element]. The size of the nucleus and the individual electrons are tiny compared to the overall size of the atom. If an atom were the size of an athletics stadium, the nucleus would be the size of a pea at its center, and the electrons would be the size of grains of sand in the surrounding stands." [3]

Electrons are inconceivable.
Here's more magic from the world of the very small: "Electrons are not like orbiting planets [around a nucleus], but more like the blades of a spinning fan, managing to fill every bit of space in their orbits simultaneously (but with the crucial difference that the blades of the fan only *seem* to be everywhere at once; electrons *are*)."

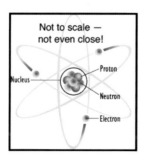

Sources:
[1] *Spectrums*, p. 49.
[2] *A Short History* . . ., pp. 140-41.
[3] Miodownik, Mark. *Stuff Matters*. 2013, Mariner Books: Boston, p. 148.
[4] *A Short History* . . ., p. 141.
Photo: Atom diagram (Wikimedia Commons – Google Creative Commons)

WONDER 13 -- Forces

Atoms are almost entirely empty space. So why aren't all materials transparent? And why can't we walk through a wall? Answers below.

Is gravity a strong force? No!

There are four basic forces in nature. The Strong Force binds atomic nuclei together. It is 137 times stronger than the next strongest force, Electromagnetism (the force between charged particles). The Strong Force is one million times stronger than the Weak Force, which acts in radioactive decay. And the Strong Force is ten billion billion billion (10^{28}) times stronger than gravity, which is not as strong as a small magnet. [1]

When you sit in a chair, you are not touching the chair but are levitating one angstrom above it.

Objects that appear to be touching are not actually touching, thanks to repelling forces between atoms.
When two billiard balls come together, they don't actually strike each other. Rather, the negatively charged fields of the balls repel each other. Otherwise they would pass right through each other. "When you sit in a chair, you are not actually sitting there, but levitating above it at a height of one angstrom (a hundred millionth [10^{-8}] of a centimeter), your electrons and its electrons implacably opposed to any closer intimacy." [2]

"Electromagnetic force pulls atoms into molecules and holds them together across enormous (to an atom) distances, forming what (from our size) appear to be solid objects. Without that subtle attraction, your chair, your floor, you, Earth would come apart as nothing but gas." [3]

The REAL force is within

Sources:
[1] ph.surrey.ac: "The Forces Of Nature"   https://bit.ly/3x2lYHo
[2] *A Short History . . .*, p. 141.
[3] *Spectrums*, p. 81.
Photo: Horseshoe magnet, nails (Pixabay – Google Creative Commons) [caption added]

WONDER 14 – Molecules and Atoms

If molecules of air were grains of sand, one cubic centimeter of air would contain 45 billion dump trucks of air molecules.

Air is not nothing. "At sea level, at zero degrees Celsius [32 degrees F.], one cubic centimeter of air (that is, a space about the size of a sugar cube) will contain 45 billion billion [45 x 10^{18}] molecules. And they are in every single cubic centimeter you see around you." A dump truck full of sand holds a billion grains of sand, so 45 billion of them would hold 45 billion billion grains. [1]

There are more stars in the universe than grains of sand on all the beaches, and almost as many atoms in a grain of sand as stars in the universe.

How many atoms are there in a single grain of sand? Between 50 quintillion (50 x 10^{18}) and 300 quintillion . . . or more than all the grains of sand on all the beaches and almost as many as the number of stars in the universe! [3]

Sources:
[1] *A Short History* . . ., p. 133-34.
Sciforums.com: "The best visual description of the size of one billion"   https://bit.ly/32obC6L
[2] npr.org: "Which is Greater, The Number of Sand Grains on Earth or Stars in the Sky?"
https://n.pr/3tqfZdc
[3] Quora.com: "How many atoms are there in a grain of sand?"   https://bit.ly/3dvEPmB
Photo: Starry sky (Pixabay – Google Creative Commons)

WONDER 15 – Even Smaller Things

There's small . . . and then there's strings. And neutrinos.

We'll end our look at the very, very small with two of the very, very smallest – and strangest.

A current theory of the structure of things is called string theory, according to which everything is ultimately made not of point-like particles but of "vibrating strings" that are one-dimensional (!). And very small. Their size is about one "Planck length", which is 1.6×10^{-35} m. If one atom were the size of our Solar System, one string would be the width of a strand of DNA. [1]

Neutrinos are subatomic particles that are produced in nuclear reactions on the Sun and other stars (and in nuclear reactions on Earth). They are ". . . so unbelievably small and slippery that they can travel at near the speed of light through virtually anything. Each second, the Sun releases about 2×10^{38} of these little guys (that's 200 trillion trillion trillion neutrinos each second), and about 65 billion of them end up passing through each and every square centimeter of Earth. That's trillions of neutrinos passing through you right now. It doesn't matter if it's nighttime and the Sun is shining on the other side of the planet: neutrinos can literally cruise through Earth, meandering among atoms, unaffected and unaffecting." [2]

Sources:
[1] *Spectrums*, p. 52.
[2] *Spectrums*, p.131.
Photo: Sun flares (PxHere – Google Creative Commons)

Scale: Time, Very Fast and Very Slow

The first two sections looked at redefining our sense of scale in terms of space. This section may do the same for the dimension of time.

WONDER 16 – The Very Fast

How fast is a second?

What happens in one second?
In one second "a hummingbird flaps its wings 70 times, sound travels 340 meters (1,115 ft), and a flash of light rushes past 300 million meters [186,000 mi] . . . . [O]xygen molecules at room temperature zip through the air at over 450 meters per second (1,600 km/h or 1,000 mph) . . . . Earth spins through space at about the same rate – the equator turning at about 1680 km/h [1,008 mph]." [1]

Even faster are some human inventions. "In a single second, a communication satellite, traversing the sky 36,000 km (22,000 miles) above sea level in a round-each-day geosynchronous orbit, travels 3,100 meters in a second (11,160 km/h or 6,900 mph). The space shuttle was twice as fast, accelerating from 0 to 17,000 mph (27,360 km/h) in just over 8 minutes." [1]

Still faster are radio signals. "[I]f radio signals could bend, they could travel around the globe 7 times each second." [2] That's more than 174,000 miles (279,000 km) per second. That's close to the speed of light –186,000 miles (297,600 km) per second – which makes sense because radio waves are a type of light.

How fast is a microsecond? How about a nanosecond?

A microsecond is one millionth of a second.
"A microsecond is to a single second what 1 second is to 11.5 days – in other words, if you took one step each second, you'd have to walk for 277 hours

51

straight to reach a million. To give you a sense of how long (well, short) a microsecond is, it takes about 500,000 microseconds to click a mouse. And yet, because sound reaches one of our ears just 600 microseconds before the other, we can identify where it originated and turn our head to it, even with our eyes closed." [3]

As brief as a microsecond is, "A lot can happen in even a single microsecond: Earth orbits another 18.5 millimeters (about ¾ in), light travels 300 meters (1,000 ft) . . . ." [3]

A nanosecond is a *billionth* of a second. "[A] microprocessor inside a desktop computer takes just a few nanoseconds to carry out an instruction, such as adding two numbers. In the time it takes you to blink your eye, a typical computer can do 900 million calculations." [4] These computer tasks are subdivided into smaller pieces-- "flops" (floating point operations per second). Quadrillions (10^{15}) of these flops can be carried out each second! [5]

Sources:
[1] *Spectrums*, p. 144.
[2] *Spectrums*, p.67.
[3] *Spectrums*, p. 155.
[4] *Spectrums*, p. 156.
[5] *Spectrums*, p. 15.
Photo: Heuer stopwatch (Wikimedia Commons – Google Creative Commons)

WONDER 17 – The Very Slow

Age of Earth and the Universe

When we talk about things happening slowly, we often use the term "geologic time". This refers to the age of Earth, or about 4.5 billion years during which the Earth formed, continents moved and changes took place resulting in our present planet. How slow has that process been?

"Imagine that a single year is represented by a 1-millimeter (3/64 in) length of string; a century is 10 centimeters (about 4 in), a millennium is 1 meter (39 in). To demonstrate the age of Earth, you would need a string that spans from San Francisco to New York." [1]

Imagine again: this time "[I]magine a time-lapse where each frame captures a moment every ten thousand years. If we started shooting at the birth of the planet, the finished movie (to the current day, at least) would be four hours long, and the entire history of the human species wouldn't show up until well into the final one second of footage." [2] (More about how long humans have been on Earth compared to the life of the planet in a later wonder.)

The age of the universe is estimated to be 13.8 billion years, so it existed for more than 8 billion years before Earth was formed. [3] It's kind of sobering to think that there was a universe *without* Earth for much longer than there has been a universe *with* Earth.

Sources:
[1] *Spectrums*, p. 145.
[2] *Spectrums*, p. 146.
[3] USA Today (7/15/20): "Universe is 13.8 billion years old, scientists confirm"
https://bit.ly/2Qhfe7T

THE LIVING WORLD

Living Things – Numbers and Variety

We typically do not *see* great numbers of any one type of animal, except maybe when ants invade our homes or mosquitoes disrupt our picnics. And we do not see a great *variety* of animals except when we visit the zoo. We do see a lot of plants -- fields of wild or cultivated grasses, grains or vegetables; forests of trees – but again, not a great variety. How many different species of animals and plants are there? How many species of particular kinds of animals, and how numerous are the individuals in those species? How about living things we cannot see, such as viruses and bacteria: how varied and numerous are they? What do we know about living things below ground level?

WONDER 18 – Numbers and Biomass of Living Things

What are the most numerous animals on Earth? How much do they weigh as a group?

Among mammals, chickens (around 20 billion) and rats (uncounted, but estimated to be over 8 billion) outnumber humans (7.9 billion). Among large mammals we are most numerous, followed by cattle (1.4 billion) and sheep (1.1 billion), but cattle have greater total biomass than humans, more than 500 billion tons compared to our 350 billion tons.

Among all animals, the most numerous and massive groupings are bacteria, with 5 quadrillion quadrillion or 5 noniliion (10^{30}) individuals and biomass equal to one trillion (10^{12}) tons; followed by ants (10 billion billion or 10 quintillion (10^{18}); 3 billion tons), marine fish (800 million; 2 billion tons), cattle (520 million tons), termites (445 million tons), humans (7.9 billion; 350 million tons), Antarctic krill (500 trillion; 150 million tons), and sheep (1.1 billion; 65 million tons).

So, excluding microbes (bacteria, fungi, algae, protozoa and viruses), the number one species in population is Antarctic krill, with 500 trillion – or perhaps the bristlemouth, a vertebrate fish (see Wonder 45 below). And #1 in biomass is ants, with 3 billion tons.

For large groupings of living things, the total biomass of terrestrial plants is 560 billion tons; of marine plants is 5-10 billion tons; and of terrestrial animals is 5 billion tons. Again, all that is dwarfed by bacteria: one trillion (10^{12}) tons.

WONDER 19 – Numbers of Species

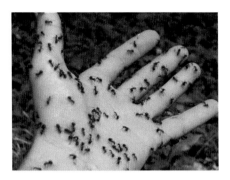

Of the estimated 8.7 million species of life on Earth, scientists have named and catalogued only 1.3 million of them.

"Scientists have named and cataloged 1.3 million species. How many more species there are left to discover is a question that has hovered like a cloud over the heads of taxonomists for two centuries. 'It's astounding that we don't know the most basic thing about life,' said Boris Worm, a marine biologist at Dalhousie University in Nova Scotia. [Dr. Worm] and colleagues . . . estimate there are 8.7 million species on the planet, plus or minus 1.3 million." [1]

There is only one existing species of humans today, *Homo sapiens.* How does that stack up against other animals?

Number of species: ants

"We share the Earth with an estimated 1 quadrillion [10^{15}] ants spread out over more than 12,000 ant species. That's 1,000,000,000,000,000 of these insects." [2]

Numbers of species: microbes (bacteria, fungi, algae, amoebae)

There are roughly 5,000 species of bacteria; 26,900 species of algae; 70,000 species of fungi; 30,800 species of amoebae and related organisms. [3] Another estimate puts the number of known species of bacteria at roughly 30,000. [4]

Numbers of species: lichens

"[Lichens] are . . . a partnership between fungi and algae. The fungi excrete acids which dissolve the surface of [a] rock, freeing minerals that the algae convert into food sufficient to sustain them both. It is not a very exciting

57

arrangement, but it is a conspicuously successful one. The world has more than 20,000 species of lichens." [5]

Sources:
[1] Zimmer, Carl. "How Many Species?" NY Times, August 23, 2011
[2] https://ants.com
[3] *A Short History* . . ., p. 309.
[4] Dykhuizen, Daniel. "Species Numbers in Bacteria", <u>Proceedings of California Academy of Sciences</u>, June 3, 2005; 56960, pp. 62-71.
[5] *A Short History* . . ., p. 336.
Photo: Ants on hand (Max Pixel – Google Creative Commons)

WONDER 20 – Microbes

Bacteria: numerous, tiny and diverse

Microbes are microscopic organisms. They are very, very numerous. Because they are so small, they don't weigh much, and yet "If you totaled up all the biomass of the planet – every living thing, plants included – microbes would account for at least 80 per cent of all there is, perhaps more." [1]

Scientists estimate that there are five quadrillion quadrillion (or 5 nonillion) (5 x 10^{30}) bacteria on Earth. That's *more* than the number of stars in the universe or grains of sand on Earth's beaches! [2]

A bacterium weighs "about one trillionth of the weight of a dollar bill and lives for no more than twenty minutes." [3]

Another indication of their minuteness, referring to *E. Coli* bacteria: "In their world, even pure water is as thick as honey . . . . About 200,000 of these little creatures could live in the period at the end of this sentence." [4]

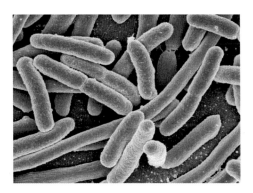

Sources:
[1] *A Short History . . .*, p. 311-12.
[2] sciencing.com: "How Many Bacteria Live on Earth?"   https://bit.ly/3tuzZvt
[3] Bryson, Bill. *The Body: A Guide for Occupants.* 2019, Doubleday: New York, p. 29.
[4] *Spectrums*, p. 47.
Photo: E. coli bacteria (Max Pixels – Google Creative Commons)

WONDER 21 – Extinction

Most species from the past are now extinct, huge numbers are unknown/undescribed, and the number of annual extinctions is unknown, but may be alarmingly high.

We don't hear much about extinctions. They happen in the background of our lives, unless a species we know and love is about to become extinct. Extinctions are more frequent than we might imagine.

"More than 99 percent of all species, amounting to over five billion species, that ever lived on Earth are estimated to be extinct. Estimates of the number of Earth's current species range from 10 million to 14 million, of which about 1.2 million have been documented and over 86 percent have not yet been described . . . . [1]

There is certainly a wide range of estimates among scientists concerning species, but the trends are clear: huge numbers of species, mostly unknown, and huge numbers of extinctions.

"The rapid loss of species we are seeing today is estimated by experts to be between 1,000 and 10,000 times higher than the *natural extinction rate*. [This is the rate of extinction that would occur without humans.] These experts calculate that between 0.01% and 0.1% of all species will become extinct each year. If the low estimate of the number of species out there is true – i.e., that there are around 2 million different species on our planet – then that means between 200 and 2,000 extinctions occur every year. But if the upper estimate of species numbers is true – that there are 100 million different species co-existing with us on our planet – then between 10,000 and 100,000 species are becoming extinct each year." [2]

Sources:
[1] Wikipedia.org: "Lists of organisms by population"   https://bit.ly/3ghBOlg
[2] World Wildlife Fund (wwf.panda.org): "Well, this is the million dollar question…"
https://bit.ly/3aiZ7xG
Photo: Dodo (Wikimedia Commons – Google Creative Commons)

WONDER 22 – A Special Case: Viruses

Viruses – numbers and size

Since the beginning of the SARS-CoV-2 (COVID-19) pandemic in Spring 2019, we have learned more about viruses, or at least about that particular coronavirus. However, there is much that hasn't made the headlines.

Viruses are not living organisms. They are assemblages of proteins, nucleic acids, lipids and carbohydrates that cannot replicate unless they enter a living cell.

There are an estimated 10 nonillion (10^{30}) viruses on and in Earth – far more than the number of stars in the universe or grains of sand on Earth's beaches. [1]

"According to the virologist Dorothy H. Crawford, ocean viruses alone if laid end to end would stretch for ten million light-years, a distance essentially beyond imagining." [2]

Phages are a type of virus that attack bacteria. "Phages are the largest category of viruses in nature. Indeed, phage viruses are by far the most plentiful biological entity on earth. There are 10^{31} of them – a trillion phages for every grain of sand, and more than all organisms (including bacteria) combined." [3]

We have seen that bacteria are tiny, so how do viruses compare with them in size – and how do both compare with us?
"If a virus was [expanded to the] size of a five-cent coin, a bacterium would be the size of a dinner plate, and you [expanded proportionately] would be 200 kilometres [125 mi] tall!" [4]

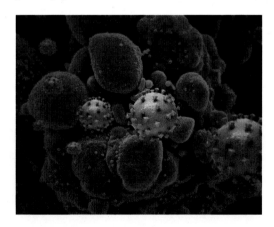

Sources:

[1] nationalgeographic.com: "There are more viruses than stars in the universe. Why do only some infect us?"   https://bit.ly/3twwOTN

[2] *The Body*, p. 33.

[3] Isaacson, Walter. *The Code Breaker: Jennifer Doudna, Gene Editing, and the Future of the Human Race*. 2021. Simon & Schuster: New York, p. 75.

[4] ABC Science "Bernie's Basics – The big and the small"   https://ab.co/3aTBFau

Photo: Creative rendition of SARS Coronavirus (Flickr – Google Creative Commons)

WONDER 23 – The Ground Beneath Our Feet

Living things in a spoonful of soil

"A single spoonful of soil may contain *10,000 different species* of bacteria, many of which are new to science." [1]

"A single spadeful of rich garden soil contains more species of organisms than can be found above ground in the entire Amazon rain forest." [2]

"Every time you take a step in a mature Oregon forest, your foot is being supported on the backs of 16,000 invertebrates held up by an average total of 120,000 legs." (Dr. Andrew Moldenke, Oregon State University) [2]

"One cupful of undisturbed native soil may contain: 200 billion bacteria, 20 million protozoa, 100,000 nematodes, 50,000 arthropods, and 100,000 meters [328,000 ft] of fungi." [3]

From E.O. Wilson, Pulitzer Prize-winning biologist nicknamed "The New Darwin":
"So far, about 60,000 species of fungi have been discovered and studied, including mushrooms, rusts and molds. But specialists estimate that more than 1.5 million species exist on Earth. Along with them in the soil thrive some of the most abundant animals in the world, the nematodes, also known as roundworms. Tens of thousands of roundworm species are known, and the true number could be in the millions. Both fungi and roundworms are outdone dramatically in turn by still smaller organisms. In a pinch of garden soil, about a gram in weight, live millions of bacteria, representing several thousand species. Most of them are unknown to science." [4]

Who knew the ground we walk upon was so rich in life?!

It is estimated that there are 3.04 trillion trees on Earth, or 420 per person (not to imply any sort of ownership, of course). That's about the same number as have been cut down since the last ice age 11,000 years ago. Today's rate of tree slaughter is 15 billion per year, or 41 million per day. [5]

Here are a couple more revelations about the world beneath our feet. The tips of small plant roots move through the soil with a twisting screw-like motion. Mature trees can have as many as 5 million active root tips. [6]

"The plants growing in a 2-acre wheat field can have more than 30,000 miles [48,000 km] of roots, greater than the circumference of the Earth." [7]

Living things in the soil: mycorrhizae

Mycelium is the vegetative (underground) part of any fungus, consisting of microscopic hairs (hyphae). When they interact with tree roots, they are called mycorrhizae and allow trees to "communicate" by sharing nutrients. They are very small, especially compared to gigantic trees: as much as 7-8 miles in a cubic inch of soil. [8]

Living things in the soil: bacteria

"Some scientists now think that there could be as much as 100 trillion tons of bacteria living beneath our feet in what are known as subsurface lithoautotrophic microbial ecosystems – SLiME for short. Thomas Gold of Cornell University has estimated that if you took all the bacteria out of the Earth's interior and dumped them on the surface, they would cover the planet to a depth of 15 meters [49 ft] – the height of a four-story building. If the estimates are correct, there could be more life under the Earth than on top of it." [9]

The soil breathes!

"Although the soil surface appears solid, air moves freely in and out of it. The air in the upper 8 inches [20 cm] of a well-drained soil is completely renewed about every hour." [10]

Sources:
[1] Zimmer, Carl. "How Many Species?" NY times, August 23, 2011.
[2] "Soil Biology": Natural Resources Conservation Service,
http://extension.illinois.edu/soil/sb_mesg/sb_mesg.htm
[3] Colorado State University Extension: "The Living Soil"   https://bit.ly/2QeJyjt

[4] Wilson, E. O. "Within One Cubic Foot", National Geographic Magazine, February 2010.
[5] http://www.bbc.com/news/science-environment-34134366
[6] http://extension.illinois.edu/soil/sb_mesg/sb_mesg.htm
[7] Natural Resources Conservation Service: "Soil Biology"   https://bit.ly/3v1wAEu
[8] Radiolab (wnycstudios.org): "From Tree to Shining Tree"   https://bit.ly/3gksKCp
[9] *A Short History* . . ., p. 305.
[10] University of Illinois Extension – "Soil Biology"   https://bit.ly/3nJ0OtB
Photo: Handful of soil (Flickr – Google Creative Commons)

WONDER 24 – The Miracle of Growth

Weight of a redwood tree compared to weight of its seed

The largest tree on Earth, the General Sherman sequoia in California's Sequoia National Park, weighs about 6,167 tons (12.3 million lbs or 5.6 million kg). A sequoia seed is so small that 3,000 of them weigh about 1 ounce. The trunk of the tree alone increased in weight over 58 billion times during its growth.

Source:
National Park Service (nps.gov): "A short history of a long-lived tree"   https://bit.ly/3ghE16w
Britannica (Britannica.com): "General Sherman"   https://bit.ly/3aktfbZ
Photo: General Sherman sequoia (Flickr – Google Creative Commons)

Evolution and Humans

This section narrows the focus of living things to humans, with many surprising revelations about how we got here, and when; and how interrelated we are across space and time.

WONDER 25 – Age of Earth and Humans' Time Upon It

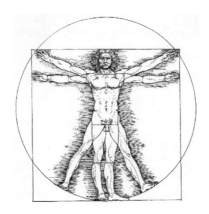

Earth is old, and the universe much older – and we and other life forms are very young.

The earth is 4,600,000,000 years old. If that period were graphically represented by the fingertip-to-fingertip distance of your arms outstretched to the side, and if Earth began at your left fingertip:
• one-celled life forms appear somewhere between your left wrist and elbow (and continue to the present);
• just past your right shoulder, two-celled life forms appear;
• at your right wrist, animals with hard body parts appear;
• dinosaurs existed between the joints of your right fingers;
And humans? Take a nail file and gently scrape the nail of your right middle finger: you've just removed all of human history. [1]

Here's another way of understanding the same chronology:
"Let's imagine that "Mother Earth" is celebrating her 50th birthday right now – that is, her whole 4.5 billion years were compressed down into 50. In that case, the first signs of simple life don't show up until she was age 11. The first animals with eyes (such as trilobites and horseshoe crabs) appeared just before her 45th birthday. Dinosaurs went extinct a few months after she turned 49. *Homo erectus* (Java man) learned to control fire this week, and *Homo sapiens* showed up yesterday. The last major ice age ended an hour ago, and civilization – virtually all our recorded history, art, and science – began a few

minutes later. Jesus was born a little over 10 minutes ago. And the age of modern computers began 17 seconds ago. Happy birthday, Mom." [2]

And here's yet a third analogy, this time going all the way back to the beginning of the universe:

"Consider [astronomer] Carl Sagan's famous 'cosmic calendar,' on which the history of the universe is compacted into a single solar year. At this scale, the universe began on January 1, the Milky Way started forming in March, though our Sun and Earth weren't born until September 1. Later that month, single-celled creatures appeared, followed sometime in November by multicellular organisms. Mammals appeared on December 26. Dinosaurs were wiped out on December 29. All human prehistory (from the first known stone tools) and history occurred during the final hour of New Year's Eve, and our entire recorded history of civilization takes up just the last 22 seconds of the last minute of December 31." [3]

Evolutionary longevity – trilobites (vs. humans)

Trilobites were a prehistoric arthropod similar in appearance to modern horseshoe crabs, that lived from around 500-200 million years ago. "Trilobites . . . reigned for 300 million years – twice the span of dinosaurs, which were themselves among history's great survivors. Humans . . . have survived so far for one-half of 1 per cent as long." [4] [5]

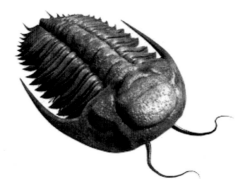

Sources:
[1] Several sources, including:
jersey.uoregon.edu: "How long has the earth been here?"   https://bit.ly/3aol5zk
McPhee, John. *Basin and Range.* 1981, Farrar Straus: New York, p. 126
[2] *Spectrums*, p. 149-50.
[3] *Spectrums*, p. 151.
[4] *A Short History . . .*, p. 323.
Photo: DaVinci's Vitruvian Man (Wikimedia Commons – Google Creative Commons); Trilobite (Wikimedia Commons – Google Creative Commons)

WONDER 26 – Earth Itself is Changing

The present location of land masses on Earth is the way it has been for only one-tenth of one percent of Earth's history.

Earth's land masses have been – and still are – on the move.

"The connections between modern land masses and those of the past were found to be infinitely more complex than anyone had imagined. Kazakhstan, it turns out, was once attached to Norway and New England. One corner of Staten Island, but only a corner, is European . . . . The Scottish Highlands and much of Scandinavia are substantially American. Some of the Shackleton Range of Antarctica, it is thought, may once have belonged to the Appalachians of the eastern US. Rocks, in short, get around . . . . Look at a globe and what you are seeing really is a snapshot of the continents as they have been for just one-tenth of 1 per cent of the Earth's history."

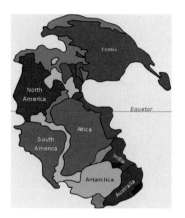

Source:
A Short History . . ., p. 181-82.
Photo: Pangaea (Wikimedia Commons – Google Creative Commons)

WONDER 27 – The Magic of Evolution

There was no first human being.

Who was the first person, the first *Homo sapiens*? Answer: there wasn't one. How is this possible? Given that the definition of a species is the capability of mating and producing viable offspring that can also reproduce, every one of our ancestors had parents of the same species and gave birth to offspring of the same species. And yet, going back 185 million generations, our ancestor was a fish! As Richard Dawkins states: "There never was a *Homo erectus* [our human ancestor just prior to *Homo sapiens*] who suddenly gave birth to a *Homo sapiens* baby." [1]

The solution to understanding this conundrum is *time*: the changes from generation to generation were small, but there were 185 million small changes. It's like changes in our own lifetimes: "There never comes a day when you can say 'This person has suddenly stopped being a child and become an adolescent' . . . . Nobody would ever want to call your fishy 185-millions-greats-grandfather a man . . . even though there is a continuous chain linking him to you, every link in the chain being a member of exactly the same species as its neighbours in the chain." [2]

Heady stuff indeed.

Sources:
[1] Dawkins, Richard. *The Magic of Reality*. 2011, Free Press: New York, chapter 2.
[2] The New Yorker Festival (10/14/2011): "Richard Dawkins: Who was the first human?" (YouTube)   https://bit.ly/3e9SqiA
Photo: Man holding tuna (PxFuel – Google Creative Commons)

WONDER 28 – Fossils

Only about one bone in a billion becomes fossilized, and only one species in 120,000 is in the fossil record.

"It isn't easy to become a fossil. The fate of nearly all living organisms – over 99.9% of them – is to compost down to nothingness . . . . Only about one bone in a billion . . . ever becomes fossilized. If that is so, it means that the complete fossil legacy of all the Americans alive today – that's 270 million people with 206 bones each – will only be about 50 bones, one-quarter of a complete skeleton. That's not to say, of course, that any of these bones will ever actually be found . . . . Most of what has lived on earth has left behind no record at all. It has been estimated that less than one species in 120 thousand has made it into the fossil record." [1]

All of the fossil remains of prehistoric humans would fit in the back of a pickup truck.

"Since the dawn of time, several billion human (or humanlike) beings have lived . . . . Out of this vast number, the whole of our understanding of human prehistory is based on the remains, often exceedingly fragmentary, of perhaps five thousand individuals. 'You could fit it all into the back of a pickup truck' [Ian Tattersall, curator of anthropology, American Museum of Natural History] . . . ."

Homo erectus lived on Earth for over a million years, inhabiting an area from Western Europe to eastern China. "Yet if you brought back to life every *Homo erectus* individual whose existence we can vouch for [from fossil remains], they wouldn't fill a school bus . . . . Something as short-lived as our own civilization would almost certainly not be known from the fossil record at all." [2]

Sources:
[1] *A Short History . . .*, p. 321-22.
[2] *A Short History . . .*, p. 440-41.
Photo: Pickup truck (Public Domain Pictures – Google Creative Commons)

WONDER 29 – Number of Human Ancestors

Going back to the time of the Romans, each of us has approximately one million trillion ancestors.

"If your two parents hadn't bonded just when they did – possibly to the second, possibly to the nanosecond – you wouldn't be here. And if their parents hadn't . . . you wouldn't be here either. And if their parents . . . . Push backwards through time and these ancestral debts begin to add up. Go back just eight generations to about the time that Charles Darwin and Abraham Lincoln were born [on the same day!], and already there are over 250 people on whose timely couplings your existence depends. Continue further, to the time of Shakespeare and the Mayflower pilgrims, and you have no fewer than 16,384 ancestors earnestly exchanging genetic material in a way that would, eventually and miraculously, result in you."

Go back 20 generations and the number of your ancestors is 1,048,576! Go back 25 generations and there are "no fewer than 33,554,432 men and women on whose devoted couplings your existence depends." Go back to the time of the Romans and the number is approximately one million trillion – many, many times more than the total number of people who have ever lived!

The answer to this paradox? "Incest . . . at a genetically discreet remove. With so many millions of ancestors in your background, there will have been many occasions when a relative from your mother's side of the family procreated with some distant cousin from your father's side of the ledger."

Source:
A Short History . . ., p. 397-98.
Photo: Abraham Lincoln (Wikimedia Commons – Google Creative Commons)

WONDER 30 – We're All Related

Most of the people you see in any group of people around you are probably relatives.

"[If] you are in a partnership now with someone from your own race and country, the chances are excellent that you are at some level related. Indeed, if you look around you on a bus or in a park or café or any crowded place, *most* of the people you see are very probably relatives. When someone boasts to you that he is descended from Shakespeare . . . you should answer at once: 'Me, too!' In the most literal and fundamental sense we are all family." [1]

Up to a billion of our atoms once belonged to Shakespeare.

Atoms are durable. "Every atom you possess has almost certainly passed through several stars and been part of millions of organisms on its way to becoming you. We are each so atomically numerous and so vigorously recycled at death that a significant number of our atoms – up to a billion for each of us . . . – probably once belonged to Shakespeare. A billion more each came from Buddha and Genghis Khan and Beethoven [or Jesus], and any other historical character you care to name . . . . So we are all reincarnations . . . ." [2]

"Every time you breathe, you exhale some 25 sextillion (that's 2.5×10^{22}) molecules of oxygen – so many that with a day's breathing you will in all likelihood inhale at least one molecule from the breaths of every person who has ever lived. And every person who lives from now on until the Sun burns out will from time to time breathe in a bit of you. At the atomic level, we are in a sense eternal." [3]

Sources:
[1] *A Short History . . .*, p. 398.
[2] *A Short History . . .*, p. 134.
[3] *The Body*, p.212.
Photo: William Shakespeare (Flickr – Google Creative Commons)

74

WONDER 31 – We're All Similar

We humans have very little genetic variability.

" 'There's more genetic variability in one social group of fifty-five chimps than in the entire human population', as one authority has put it . . . . Because we are recently descended from a small foundling population [no more than a few thousand individuals], there hasn't been time enough or people enough to provide a source of great variability." [1]

"The paradox of genetics is that we are all very different and yet genetically practically identical. All humans share 99.9 percent of their DNA, and yet no two humans are alike. My DNA and your DNA will differ in three to four million places, which is a small proportion of the total but enough to make a lot of difference between us. You also have within you about a hundred personal mutations – stretches of genetic instructions that don't quite match any of the genes given to you by either of your parents but are yours alone." [2]

Because they have been around for so long, "[T]wo strains of *E. coli* have more genetic variability than all the mammals on Earth put together." [3]

Sources:
[1] *A Short History* . . ., p. 463.
[2] *The Body*, p. 7.
[3] *The Body*, p. 258.
Photo: Chimpanzees (Public Domain Pictures – Google Creative Commons)

The Human Body

We are little aware of what goes on inside our bodies. Wonders abound, many requiring us to consider the world of the very, very small. The wonder that launched this book is here: the strand of DNA that is inside each of our microscopic 37 trillion cells is over three feet [1 m] long. That's *very* small – and thin! This section also broaches what other living things inhabit our bodies and what it really means to be human if we host such a menagerie.

WONDER 32 – Number of Cells and Atoms

The building blocks of our bodies are incredibly small and numerous.

We tend to think of our bodies as made up of organs – these are what we are *aware* of, when they work, surreptitiously and silently, but especially when they hurt or don't work. However, they are the mega-constructions: dig deeper, focus finer and you find the almost infinitesimal building blocks.

How many cells comprise a human body? Hmm, somewhere between 37.2 trillion [1] and 100 trillion (10^{14}) [2]. That's quite a range, but it underscores that whatever the actual number is, it's very, very large.

Going to the tiniest level, how many *atoms* are in the human body? In a person of average weight (70 kg/154 lbs), we are composed of 7×10^{27} (7 octillion, or 7 followed by 27 zeros) atoms. [3]
Of that humongous number, about 2/3 are hydrogen atoms, 1/4 oxygen, 1/10 carbon. [4]

Put another way, "Each cell in the human body contains more atoms than there are stars in the Milky Way." [5]

And a dramatic analogy to sum it up:
"If you magnified everything so that an apple appeared as large as our Earth, a flea would be the size of a small country, and an amoeba or a human body cell would be the size of a midsized city. A human chromosome would be the size of a baseball field, a virus would fit inside the infield, and a single molecule would fit on home plate." [6]

Sources:
[1] *The Body* . . ., p. 9
[2] *Spectrums,* p. 19.
[3] *Spectrums*, p. 20 and *The Body*, p. 5.
[4] JLab Science Education: "How many atoms are in the human body?"   https://bit.ly/32ngxoi
[5] *Spectrums,* p. 16.
[6] *Spectrums,* p. 49.
Photo: Apple and Earth (Pixabay – Google Creative Commons)

WONDER 33 – Blood

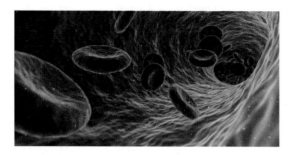

Our blood is something we notice at a small level. If we see a speck of blood on our skin or on a tissue, we notice. But of course, that is still macro, not micro. How many blood cells do we have, and how small are they?

There are about 25 trillion red blood cells/corpuscles in the average human body. [1]

"If a red blood cell were expanded to the size of an apple, an apple enlarged the same amount would be twice as tall as the Empire State Building." [2]

Red blood cells circulate through blood vessels, carrying oxygen throughout our bodies via molecules of the protein hemoglobin.
"Within your modest frame are some twenty-five thousand miles [40,233 km] of blood vessels [mostly capillaries] . . . ." [3] That's slightly more than the circumference of Earth (24,901 mi/40,074 km).

Our blood whizzes around our circulatory system. It takes about a minute for a molecule of oxygen to enter our nostrils, be circulated through our bodies in hemoglobin (in red blood cells), be exchanged for carbon dioxide, and exit the mouth or nose. "Inside each of our 25 trillion red blood cells are 270 million molecules of hemoglobin, each of which has room for four oxygen molecules. That's *a billion molecules of oxygen* boarding and disembarking within each red blood cell cruise ship." [4]

Each red blood corpuscle "survives for about four months . . . . Each will be shot around your body about 150,000 times, logging a hundred miles or so of travel before it is too battered to go on . . . . You discard about a hundred billion red blood cells every day. They are a big part of what makes your stools brown." [5]

Sources:
[1] Wikipedia – "Red blood cell"
[2] *Spectrums*, p. 47.

[3] *The Body,* p. 126.
[4] Nestor, James. *Breath: The New Science of a Lost Art.* 2020, Riverhead Books (Random House): New York, p. 74.
[5] *The Body,* p. 126.
Photo: Red blood cells (Wikimedia Commons – Google Creative Commons)

WONDER 34 – Other Body Parts

Some of our organs are surprisingly large.

Our skin is our largest organ, because it is stretched out, not folded. An average adult has roughly 20 square feet of skin, "but about a thousand square feet of [heavily folded] lung tissue containing about fifteen hundred miles of airways." [1]

We have about 500 million alveoli (oxygen-exchange sacs) in our lungs. [2]

"Your lungs, smoothed out, would cover a tennis court, and airways within them would stretch nearly from coast to coast. [3]

And for the men: the epididymides, the two coiled tubules in the scrotal sac that carry sperm from each testis are each 12 meters long [40 ft] or the length of a Greyhound bus. [4]

Finally, something we are rarely aware of but which is a constant presence. Because we live on the surface of Earth, underneath 60 miles [96 km] of atmosphere, we experience almost 15 pounds of air pressure on every part of our body (most directly on our head). We do not feel this pressure because air and fluids inside our body push back with the same pressure. [5]

Sources:
[1] *The Body,* p. 216.
[2] *Breath,* p. 73.
[3] *The Body,* p.5.
[4] *The Body,* p. 287.
[5] Chron ("Sciguy"): Eric Berger, 10/25/2012, "Why aren't you crushed by air pressure?" https://bit.ly/3gfHHWq
Photo: Tennis court (Public Domain Pictures – Google Creative Commons)

WONDER 35 – DNA

The most remarkable body part?

"The most remarkable part of all is possibly your DNA (or deoxyribonucleic acid) [which carries our genetic instructions for growth and development]. You have a meter [3 ft] of it packed into every cell, and so many cells [37 trillion] that if you formed all the DNA in your body into a single strand, it would stretch ten billion miles [16 billion km], to beyond Pluto. Think of it: there is enough of you to leave the solar system. You are in the most literal sense cosmic . . . . You would need twenty billion strands of DNA laid side by side to make the width of the finest human hair. Every cell in your body (strictly speaking every cell with a nucleus) holds two copies of your DNA. That's why you have enough to stretch to Pluto and beyond." [1]

If all of the DNA in all of your cells were stretched end to end, it would extend from Earth to the Moon and back almost 1,500 times, and would extend from Earth to the Sun and back about 4 times. [2]

Sources:
[1] *The Body*, p. 5-6.
Also:
wikibooks.org: "Cell biology/Introduction/Cell size"   https://bit.ly/2P0aLWJ
Smithsonian Magazine (10/24/2013): Rose Eveleth, "There are 37.2 Trillion Cells in Your Body"
https://bit.ly/3aj34m0
[2] wowreally.blog: "Your DNA would reach the moon"   https://bit.ly/3mZ5lrl
Photo: Yardstick (Flickr – Google Creative Commons)

WONDER 36 – Are We Us or Them?

We think of ourselves as individual human beings, human from head to toe. And yet, each of us is also home to an astounding number of non-human living things, without which we would not be human.

More than half of the cells in our bodies are bacteria.

"[E]ach of us contains about thirty trillion human cells and between thirty and fifty trillion bacterial cells . . . . [L]ooked at genetically, you have about twenty thousand genes of your own within you, but perhaps as many as twenty million bacterial genes, so from that perspective you are roughly 99 percent bacterial and not quite 1 percent you." [1]

The human body consists of about 30-37 trillion cells. About 300 million cells die every minute and roughly the same number are created. However, there are about 39 trillion *bacteria* (non-human) cells in our bodies. In effect, we are more than 50% non-human. Of course, 7% of our DNA is the same as that of a bacterium, so could we say that bacteria are 7% human? [2]

"If you are in good health and averagely diligent about hygiene, you will have a herd of about one billion bacteria grazing on your fleshy plains – about a hundred thousand of them on every square centimeter of skin. They are there to dine off the ten billion or so flakes of skin you shed every day, plus all the tasty oils and fortifying minerals that seep out from every pore and fissure. You are for them, the ultimate buffet . . . ." [3]

"You have about 100,000 microbes per square centimeter of skin." They consist of about 200 different species. [4]

The fascinating Belly Button Biodiversity Project (NYU, 2007) reported that belly button swabs of 60 random Americans showed "2,368 species of bacteria, 1,458 of which were unknown to science . . . an average of 24.3 [kinds of] new-to-science microbes in every navel." [5]

And our microbe "guests" inhabit more than just our navels, of course.
"[Y]ou are likely to have something like 40,000 species of microbes calling you home – 900 in your nostrils, 800 more on your inside cheeks, 1,300 next door on your gums, as many as 36,000 in your gastrointestinal tract . . . ." [6]

And there are viruses in us as well. "[T]he average person harbored 174 species of virus, 90 percent of which had never been seen before." [7]

Finally, to further confuse our identity, we change at the cellular level over time.

"[O]ur entire blood supply is re-created anew every three months, our skin replaced every two weeks; in fact, every cell in our body is replaced at least once each decade, and there are few molecules in us today that were with us as children!" [8]

So, who are we?!

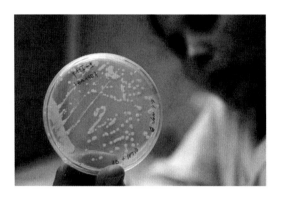

Sources:
[1] *The Body,* p. 30-31.
[2] Smithsonian Magazine (10/24/2013): Rose Eveleth, "There are 37.2 Trillion Cells in Your Body" https://bit.ly/3aj34m0
Scientific American (11/30/2007): Melinda Wenner, "Humans Carry More Bacterial Cells than Human Ones"   https://bit.ly/2QBCNbi
blogspot.com: "Why Bacteria Are Considered to be Living Organisms"   https://bit.ly/2QynMaj
[3] *A Short History* . . ., p. 302.
[4] *The Body*, p. 24-5.
[5] *The Body*, p. 25.
[6] *The Body*, p. 29-30.
[7] *The Body*, p. 33.
[8] *Spectrums*, p. 143.
Photo: Scientist holding petri dish with bacteria (Flickr – Google Creative Commons)

Animal Exceptionality, Including Us

This lengthy section introduces many wondrous animals, large and small, and their amazing traits. How do we humans stack up against these superstars? Several extraordinary animals are presented that are in a class all their own and are just too cool to ignore. And finally, human exceptionalism is explored. Just how special are we? Hubris meets humility.

WONDER 37 – The Senses: Smell, Sight, Taste, Hearing, Touch

Having looked at the amazing human body and its wonders, let's now look at the world of non-human animals (larger than microbes), through the five senses. This may help in putting human capabilities in perspective.

Amazing sense of smell: A grizzly bear can smell a carcass from 18 miles [29 km] away.

A silvertip grizzly bear can smell a carcass from 18 miles [29 km] away and can detect your presence in a place up to 48 hours after you left! A polar bear can smell a seal through three feet [1 m] of ice. Elephants, with the most olfactory receptor genes (dedicated to smell) of any animal (1,948 vs. 396 for humans) can scent water from 12 miles [19 km] away. [1]

A red-bellied newt uses its sense of smell to find its way home over a distance of two miles [3.2 km], in order to mate. [2]

Leaf-cutter ants follow scent trails. The amount of pheromones (scents) from one nest in Texas is enough to lead them three times around the world. [3]

Sources:
[1] animals.mom.com: Martha Adams, "What creature has the best sense of smell?" https://bit.ly/2QyOFuX
[2] californiaherps.com: "Red-bellied Newt: *Taricha rivularis*"   https://bit.ly/3gkMxBz
[3] tropicalecologyblog.wordpress.com: "The Importance of Pheromones as Trail Markers for Leaf-cutter Ants"   https://bit.ly/3dyB6Vr
Photo: Grizzly Bear (Public Domain Pictures – Google Creative Commons)

*Amazing sense of sight: **Eagles** can spot rabbits from several miles away.*

With eyes that have eight times the resolving power of human eyes and with 20/5 normal vision (vs. our 20/20) "Eagles can spot rabbits from several miles away while hawks and buzzards often scan the earth from a height of 10,000-15,000 feet [3,000-4,800 m] looking for tasty rodents! And when they spot one, these birds can dive at over 100 mph [160 km/h] and still keep their target in complete focus."

Sources:
allabouteyes.com: "The Best Eyes in the Animal Kingdom"   https://bit.ly/2Qdfipk
wikipedia.org: "Eagle eye"   https://bit.ly/2P2mZy4
Photo: Eagle (PxFuel – Google Creative Commons)

*Amazing sense of taste: **Catfish** have 10-15 times more tastebuds than humans.*

The animal with the most tastebuds is the catfish – 100,000-175,000. (Those who like to eat catfish already know that they have great taste.) This greatly helps them in finding small bits of food on murky river bottoms. By contrast, we humans have around 10,000 taste buds. Other mammals and their number of taste buds include dog, 1,700; cat, 500; cow, 25,000; pig, 14,000. The mammal with the fewest tastebuds is the chicken, about 30.

Amazing sense of hearing: **Moths** *and* **bats** *have much larger ranges of hearing than humans.*

The animals with the best sense of hearing are moths, bats, owls, elephants and dogs. The Greater Wax Moth can hear sound frequencies (pitches) up to 300 kHz, which gives them slightly better hearing than their main predator, bats. Humans can hear only up to 20 kHz. The normal human range of hearing, from lowest pitch to highest that we can normally hear, is 20 Hz-20 kHz, whereas the little brown bat has a range from 10.3 Hz-115 kHz. Other animals that can hear much lower pitches than we can include elephants (17 Hz) and blue whales (7 Hz). Some animals that can hear higher pitches are dogs (44 kHz), cats (64 kHz), horses (33.5 kHz), and blue whales (35 kHz). [1] [2] [3] [4]

A fish, the American shad, can also hear very high frequency sound, up to 180 kHz. [5]

So elephants and whales can hear both lower pitches and higher pitches than humans. Other animals with broader ranges of hearing than humans include horses, dolphins, rats and pigeons.

With their ability to hear very low-pitched (low frequency) sounds that travel far, an elephant can recognize a familiar elephant voice from a mile away and whales can hear the rumbling call of a family member hundreds of miles away! [6] [7]

Sources:
[1] hiddenhearing.co.uk: "The top 10 animals with the best hearing"   https://bit.ly/2QxEuXm
[2] Popular Science (popsci.com): "Which Animal Has the Most Extreme Sense of Hearing?"   https://bit.ly/32nNpgz
[3] Hearing Health USA: "Top 10 Animals with the Best Hearing"   https://bit.ly/2P00Pwh
[4] wikipedia.org: "Hearing range"   https://bit.ly/3dpZPLo

[5] Journal of Experimental Biology: D.M. Higgs et al. (1/1/2004), "Development of ultrasound detection in American shad (*Alosa sapidissima*)"   https://bit.ly/3e7FJEQ
[6] Animal Fact Guide: "African Elephant"   https://bit.ly/3mWPvh0
[7] Daily Mail: Philip Hoare (1/31/2018), "How a whale singing in the Caribbean can be heard by a chum 4000 miles away"   https://bit.ly/32sCTol
Photos: Greater wax moth (Flickr – Google Creative Commons); Spotted bat (Flickr – Google Creative Commons)

*Amazing sense of touch: Catfish, **seals**, moles, **manatees** and alligators have better sense of touch than humans.*

The sense of touch has been called the mother of all sensory systems. It is ancient and ubiquitous.

Catfish, with soft, sensitive skin and lines of hairs along their bodies, can detect vibrations in the earth and react to earthquakes days before humans are aware of them.

Seals' whiskers have more nerve receptors than other whiskered animals (such as cats), allowing them to detect vibrations of fish (prey) swimming 180 meters [590 ft] away, even in murky water.

The star-nosed mole, nearly blind, has a nose with almost six times the number of touch receptors as the human hand, allowing it to feel the vibrations of prey (worms) and devour them in a flash.

Manatees are the only animals whose entire bodies are covered with hairs that are just for the sense of touch, allowing them to sense changes in temperature, current, moving objects and tidal forces from considerable distances.

Alligators have thousands of sensory receptors along their jaws that can sense the location of prey through their slightest movement, making their jaws more sensitive than human fingertips. [1] [2]

Sources:
[1] Tail and Fur: "Animals with the Best Sense of Touch in the World"   https://bit.ly/3mWADiA
[2] 6senses.weebly.com: "Senses"   https://bit.ly/3tvwYuM
Photos: Seal (Flickr – Google Creative Commons); Manatee (Wikimedia Commons – Google Creative Commons)

WONDER 38 – Heart Rate, Breathing

Amazing heartrate: Whales and shrews are at the extremes.

 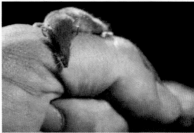

Heart rates in the animal kingdom range from blue whales, with the slowest at 8-10 beats per minute, to the Etruscan shrew, with 1,511 beats per minute. By contrast, the normal heartbeat range for humans is 60-80 (average 72) beats per minute. [1]

The slowest recorded resting human heart rate is 26 beats per minute. Olympic sprinter Usain Bolt had a resting heart rate of 30 beats per minute in peak condition. [2]

The fastest human heart rate ever recorded was 480 beats per minute. [3]

Other normal animal heart rates and ranges include: tortoise, 10 beats per minute; alligator, 32; elephant, 25-35; horse, 28-40; dairy cow, 48-84; large dog, 60-80; cat,120-140; chicken, 250-300; mouse, 450-750. [1]

Sources:
[1] Dinoanimals.com: "Heart Rates of Animals: Top 10"   https://bit.ly/3gsGISC
[2] wikipedia.org: "Bradycardia"   https://bit.ly/3sptwk5
[3] Indian Pacing and Electrophysiology Journal: Lovely Chhabra et al. (1/31/2012), "Mouse Heart Rate in a Human: Diagnostic Mystery of an Extreme Tachycardia"   https://bit.ly/3edA2oP
Photos: Blue whale (Pixabay – Google Creative Commons); Etruscan shrew (Wikimedia Commons – Google Creative Commons)

Amazing breathing: Marine mammals take the prize.

The Cuvier's beaked whale is the mammal that can hold its breath for the longest time underwater: 2 hours 17 minutes. The record for humans, held by freediver Aleix Segura Vendrell of Spain, is 24 minutes. The average for a human is 2 minutes. Average times (not records) for some other mammals: elephant seal, 2 hours; blue whale, 90 minutes; sloth, 40 minutes; beaver, 15 minutes; dolphin, 10 minutes. Sea turtles, which are reptiles, not mammals, can hold their breath for 4-7 hours.

Source:
Swim Guide: Chloe Cross, "How Long Can Mammals Hold Their Breath Underwater?"
https://bit.ly/3aovkDM
Photo: Cuvier's beaked whale (Wikimedia Commons – Google Creative Commons)

WONDER 39 – Memory

*Amazing memory: **Dolphins**, cats, elephants, ravens and even octopi have better memory than humans.*

Dolphins can remember the identifying whistles of other dolphins after 20 years of separation. [1]

A tiger's short-term memory lasts about 30 times longer than that of humans. Their brains are the largest of all carnivores (over 300 grams), and their memories are made with stronger brain synapses than humans'.

A Clark's Nutcracker, member of the raven family, can remember the exact location of up to 33,000 pine nuts it has hidden in the forest.

Elephants can keep track of the location of up to 30 family members regardless of the distance or direction of their location, using their keen sense of smell to aid with memory.

Octopi have short-term and long-term memory centers in their brains that are connected, unlike with humans, so they can ratchet up their power of memory under stress by drawing on both types of memory. [2]

Sources:
[1] National Geographic: Christine Dell'Amore (8/6/2013), "Dolphins Have Longest memories in Animal Kingdom"   https://bit.ly/3sz84c9
[2] Quora.com: "What animals have a better memory than humans?"   https://bit.ly/3dvrjPl
Photo: Dolphin (Wikimedia Commons – Google Creative Commons)

WONDER 40 – Reproductive Capacity

Amazing numbers of eggs and speed of regeneration

The ocean sunfish or mola lays up to 300 million eggs (live offspring) at one time. (Of those, two will survive to adulthood, if lucky.) Among mammals, the tenrec of Madagascar produces the largest litters, up to 32 offspring, while the naked mole rat averages 28. (Rabbits average 14.) [1]

The record for live births (that survived) among humans is eight, born to Nadya Suleman, in Bellflower, California, on January 26, 2009. [2]

Humans may have few live births, but the number of eggs (*potential* births) in the human female may surprise. "A twenty-week-old [female] fetus will weigh no more than three or four ounces but will already have six million eggs inside her. That number falls to one million by the time of birth and continues to fall, though at a slower rate, through life. As she enters her child-bearing years, a woman will have about 180,000 eggs primed and ready to go." [3]

Among insects, as with so many things, the numbers are incredible. The army ant can lay 120,000 eggs every 36 days; and queens of the African driver ant can lay 3-4 *million* eggs every 25 days! [4]

Not surprisingly, reproduction at the microbial level is at a whole different scale. "*E. coli* can reproduce seventy-two times in a day, which means that in three days they can rack up as many new generations as we have managed in the whole of human history. A single parent bacterium could in theory produce a mass of offspring greater than the weight of Earth in less than two days. In three days, its progeny would exceed the mass of the visible universe . . . . If you put all Earth's microbes in one heap and all the other animal life in another, the microbe heap would be twenty-five times greater than the animal one . . . . This is a planet of microbes. We are here at their pleasure. They don't need us at all. We'd be dead in a day without them." [5]

Sources:

[1] National Geographic: Liz Langley (4/8/2017), "These Animals Spawn the Most Offspring in One Go"   https://on.natgeo.com/32nVt0Y

[2] Wikipedia.org: "Suleman octuplets"   https://bit.ly/3grgnVn

[3] *The Body*, p. 291.

[4] University of Florida: Henning Brueland (1/15/1995), "Book of Insect Records – Chapter 18 'Highest Lifetime Fecundity' "   https://bit.ly/3n0g8Ss

[5] *The Body*, p. 29.

Photo: Ocean sunfish (Mola) (Wikimedia Commons – Google Creative Commons)

Amazing speed: A cheetah beats Usain Bolt, who ties a wombat.

When diving, the peregrine falcon can reach speeds of 240 miles per hour [386 km/h]. The human record for dive speed through the air is 822 mph [1323 km/h] – Alan Eustace, October 24, 2014 – but he started his dive at more than 25 miles [40 km] above Earth's surface (the highest recorded dive), whereas the falcon begins at around one mile [1.6 km] up.

The fastest land animal is the cheetah, with a top speed as high as 75 mph [120 km/h]. The fastest human running speed is 29.55 mph [47.56 km/h] by Olympic champion sprinter Usain Bolt during part of his record 9.58-second 100 meters race. This is about the same speed as a wombat.

Other speedy mammals include: pronghorn antelope, 55 mph [88 km/h]; mountain lion and hare, 50 mph [81 km/h]; kangaroo, 44 mph [71 km/h]. The Mexican free-tailed bat, a mammal, can fly as fast as 99 mph [159 km/h]. The fastest fish is a black marlin, 82 mph [132 km/h]. [1] [2]

Sources:
[1] National Geographic Kids: "Animal Records"   https://bit.ly/3e6d3Mg
[2] wikipedia.org: "Fastest animals"   https://bit.ly/3dvsheO
Photo: Peregrine falcon (Wikipedia – Google Creative Commons)

Amazing jumping: Humans and other mammals are not the jumping kings.

The highest-jumping mammal in relation to its body size is the klipspringer, a five-foot [1.52 m] tall antelope that can jump 10-12 feet [3-3.7 m] straight up in the air (84 inches [213 cm] above its height). With a running start, tigers can jump more than 20 feet [6 m] high. Kangaroo rats, under 4 inches [10 cm] long, can high jump 9 feet [2.7 m], or almost 30 times their body length.

The human high jump record is 8'1/4" [2.45 m] (Javier Sotomayor, 1993), although the highest jump relative to one's height was 23 inches [59 cm] above their height, by Franklin Jacobs and Stefan Holm.

The mammal long jump record is 49 feet [14.9 m] (longer than a school bus) by a snow leopard. The human record is 29'4 1/4" (8.95 m) by Mike Powell, 1991. But the real animal long jump records belong to non-mammals: grasshopper, 20 times its body length; froghopper, 70 times its body height; jumping spider, 100 times its length; tree frog, 150 times its length; flea, 220 times its length and 150 times its height! [1] [2]

Sources:
[1] National Geographic Kids: "Animal Records"   https://bit.ly/3e6d3Mg
[2] OneKind Planet: "Top 10 Highest Jumpers"   https://bit.ly/3gklkPy
Photo: Klipspringer (Wikimedia Commons – Google Creative Commons)

Amazing strength: Humans are well down the scale.

An elephant (weight up to 14,000 pounds [6,350 kg]) can carry up to 20,000 pounds [9,072 kg]. A tiger (1,200 pounds [544 kg]) can carry twice its body weight up a tree. An eagle can carry something four times its body weight during flight. A gorilla can carry 10 times its body weight. The human record for a "raw deadlift" (without special straps or suits) is 1,014 pounds [460 kg] (Benedikt Magnusson, 2014). His weight is 377 pounds [171 kg], so that lift is 2.6 times his body weight.

However, the real record holders for strength (lifting) are non-mammals: leafcutter ant, which can lift 50 times body weight; the dung beetle, capable of pulling 1,141 times its body weight; and finally, the rhinoceros beetle, which can lift 850 its times body weight. If an elephant had this strength, it could carry 850 elephants on its back and a similarly strong human could lift a 65-ton object! [1] [2]

Sources:
[1] National Geographic Kids: "Animal Records"   https://bit.ly/3e6d3Mg
[2] OneKind Planet: "Top 10 Strongest Animals"   https://bit.ly/3tuSwYz
Photo: Rhinoceros beetle (Pixabay – Google Creative Commons)

Amazing mobility: Birds are the winners.

Every year the Artic tern, a sea bird weighing less than four ounces, makes a migration of 25,000 miles (40,000 km) from its Arctic breeding grounds to the coast of Antarctica. Over its lifetime (around 25 years) a tern may cover a distance equal to three round trips from Earth to the Moon. [1]

The highest-flying animal is a Ruppell's griffon vulture, which has been recorded flying at 37,000 feet [11,277 m] altitude. About 100 humans have climbed Mt. Everest, just over 29,000 feet [8,839 m], without supplemental oxygen. Commercial planes fly at 31,000-38,000 feet [9,449-11,582 m] altitude. [2] [3] [4]

Sources:
[1] Wikipedia.org: "Arctic tern"   https://bit.ly/3efSBsn
[2] themysteriousworld.com: "Top 10 Highest Flying Birds in the World"   https://bit.ly/3tvCFZH
[3] National Geographic: "Andrew Bisharat (4/21/2016), "It's Still a Big Deal to Climb Everest Without Oxygen"   https://on.natgeo.com/3tyVQls
[4] Time: Celine Hacobian (6/27/2018), "Here's How High Planes Actually Fly, According to Experts"   https://bit.ly/3gkGRYl
Photo: Arctic tern (Flickr/Danielle Brigida – Google Creative Commons)

WONDER 42 – Anatomy

*Amazing toes: A **gecko** walking on a ceiling can support about 1,900 times its body weight hanging on its back.*

Most geckos can walk up a wall, or hang from the ceiling by a single toe. They have five toes on each foot, each with foot pads containing tiny hair-like "setae", over 6.5 million in all, each tipped with 100-1,000 spatulae that each produce a chemical reaction with molecules on a surface, allowing them to stick. Each seta is very thin, only 5 micrometers wide: nearly 1,300 would fit in the diameter of a human hair. And each spatula is one five-millionth of a meter [15 millionths of a foot] wide, "or just below the wavelength of visible light". If used all together, a 2.5-ounce [71 g] gecko on the ceiling could support a weight of 290 pounds [132 kg] (about 1,900 times its weight) hanging on its back. [1] [2]

Sources:
[1] wikipedia.org: "Gecko (Adhesion ability)"   https://bit.ly/3ehVuJz
[2] AAAS ScienceNetLinks: "Gecko Feet"   https://bit.ly/32rMrQI
Photo: Gecko (Public Domain Pictures – Google Creative Commons)

*Amazing fur: The **sea otter** has up to one million hairs per square inch of its fur.*

Sea otters have the thickest fur of any mammal: 850,000 to one million hairs per square inch [6 cm²]! That's about the size of a postage stamp. Consisting of an undercoat and longer guard hairs, this incredibly thick coat traps a layer of air next to their skin so the skin doesn't get wet. By comparison, river otters have about 300,000 hairs per square inch; cats have 60,000-120,000; dogs have 20,000-60,000; and humans have about 800 hairs per square inch on their heads.

Source:
The Marine Mammal Center: "Southern Sea Otter"   https://bit.ly/3svThPJ
Photo: Southern sea otter (Flickr – Google Creative Commons)

*Amazing jaw strength: **Sharks** and **crocs***

A great white shark probably has a bite strength of 4,000 pounds [1,814 kg] per square inch (psi) [6 cm²], although it has never been measured. Of animals that have been measured, the one with the greatest bite strength is the saltwater crocodile, 3,700 psi. With their large and powerful jaws, they can prey on cows, water buffalo, sharks and humans. Other mammals with notably powerful jaws include: jaguar, 1,500 psi; hippopotamus, 1,800 psi; gorilla, 1,300 psi; grizzly bear, 1,160 psi; hyena, 1,100 psi; tiger, 1,050 psi. By contrast, the bite strength of an average human is 162 psi. [1] [2]

Sources:
[1] Bright Side: "15+ Animals That Have the Strongest Bite"   https://bit.ly/3dq50uJ
[2] mom.com: "12 Most Powerful Bites in the Animal Kingdom"   https://bit.ly/3aiwkcf
Photos: Great white shark (Wikimedia Commons – Google Creative Commons); Saltwater crocodile (Flickr – Google Creative Commons)

WONDER 43 – Longevity

Amazing longevity – "immortal" animals

The following animals all have lifespans of 200 years or longer: ocean quahog, over 400 (record, 507); red sea urchin, bowhead whale, Aldabra tortoise, Greenland shark (record, 400 years). [1]

The longest recorded human life was just over 122.45 years (Jeanne Calment, France, 1875-1997)). [2]

The "Immortal Jellyfish", *Turritopsis dohrnii*, reacts to extreme stress by reverting to an early stage in its life development (a polyp), Benjamin Button-style, then grows again to adulthood. And on, and on, and on – so its lifespan is: ??? [3]

Flatworms can repair themselves indefinitely, with stem cells that give rise to every type of tissue – a kind of immortality. [4]

A Norway spruce with a root system 9,550 years old may support a trunk that reaches 600 years old. When the trunk dies, the root system sprouts a new tree – another kind of immortality. [5]

Of course, several plants live much longer, especially those that live in colonies. The Pando colony of quaking aspen in Utah, USA, is between 14,000 and 80,000 years old. A colony of sea grass in Spain is between 12,000 and 200,000 years old. Of individual plants, the oldest is the Methuselah bristlecone pine tree in California, at least 4,852 years old. Some aquatic species have extreme longevity. Glass sponges in the East China Sea may be more than 10,000 years old. Black coral can be more than 4,000 years old. [6]

And microorganisms have likely lived even longer. Endoliths (bacteria, fungi, lichens, algae, archaeons, amoebas living inside rocks) on the ocean floor may be millions of years old. [7]

If apparently dying and then returning to life is a kind of immortality, then consider the North American wood frog. "[It] doesn't even try to get warm when winter sets in. Instead, as the temperature drops, it suffuses its cells and bloodstream with a cocktail of sugars and proteins that allows it to freeze solid without tissue damage. Once frozen, it shows no signs of life whatsoever: no heartbeat, no breathing, no kidney function. It is as dead as a stone . . . until the spring thaw, when some deep unknown signal miraculously tells everything to start up again, and in a matter of hours the frog is hopping about looking for a mate." [8]

Tissue regeneration is another kind of immortality, perhaps. "We have organs that mostly cannot repair themselves. If a zebra fish damages its heart, it grows new tissue. If you damage your heart, well, too bad." [9]

Finally, here's an odd side note about lifespans and heart beats.

"One area where animals are curiously – almost eerily – uniform is with the number of heartbeats they have in a lifetime. Despite the vast differences in heart rates, nearly all animals have about 800 million heartbeats in them if they live an average life. The exception is humans. We pass 800 million heartbeats after twenty-five years and just keep on going for another fifty years and 1.6 billion heartbeats or so . . . . For most of our history, 800 million beats per lifetime was about the human average, too." [10]

Sources:
[1] futurelearn.com: "Lifespans of animals"   https://bit.ly/3gp7Y4y
[2] Guinness World Records: "The world's oldest people and their secrets to a long life" https://bit.ly/3v5zNmL
[3] American Museum of Natural History (5/4/2015): "The Immortal Jellyfish" https://bit.ly/3n2H9V5
Wikipedia.org: "The Curious Case of Benjamin Button" (film)   https://bit.ly/2QDFRUh
[4] Science Daily (2/27/2012): "Immortal worms defy aging"   https://bit.ly/3duigi8
[5] Scandinavian Journal of Forest Research: D. Castagneri et al. (April 2013), "Age and growth patterns of old Norway spruce trees in Trillemarka forest, Norway"   https://bit.ly/2QvXW6S
[6] OneKind Planet: "Top 10 longest living animals"   https://bit.ly/3drQaUs
[7] wikipedia.org: "List of longest-living organisms"   https://bit.ly/3gmP9yP
[8] Spectrums, p. 108.
[9] The Body, p. 9.
[10] The Body, p. 185-86.
Photo: Turritopsis dorhnii ("Immortal jellyfish") (Wikimedia Commons – Google Creative Commons)

WONDER 44 – An Extraordinary Animal: The Extremophile

Extremophiles live where no others can.

Some animals can live under extreme conditions; hence the name extremophiles. Among them: brine shrimp, which can live in water 10 times saltier than the ocean (in Great Salt Lake, for example); methane ice worms, which live on mounds of methane on the floor of the Gulf of Mexico; the "rushing fireball" microbe, which can live in boiling water; the Lazarus microbe, which can withstand 3,000 times as much radiation as humans can; sulfur-breathing bacteria; the frilly leech, which can survive being immersed in liquid nitrogen (-320 degrees Fahrenheit [-196 degrees C]) for 24 hours; the lungfish, which can live without food or water for months or even years during droughts. [1] [2]

Sources:
[1] National Geographic: Liz Langley (8/2/2013), "5 Extreme Life-Forms That Live on the Edge" https://bit.ly/3v7dptf
[2] Wikipedia.org: "Extremophile"   https://bit.ly/3dq9z8l
Photo: Brine shrimp (Wikimedia Commons – Google Creative Commons)

WONDER 45 -- An Extraordinary Animal: The Bristlemouth

The most abundant vertebrate on Earth is the ocean-dwelling bristlemouth, with millions of times more individuals than the most numerous land vertebrate.

"Scientists put the ocean's share of the biosphere at more than 99 percent. Fishermen know its surface waters and explorers its depths. But in general, compared with land, the global ocean is unfamiliar. This helps explain why scientists have only recently come to realize that the bristlemouth – a fish of the middle depths that glows in the dark and can open its mouth extraordinarily wide, baring needlelike fangs – is the most numerous vertebrate on the earth . . . . [I]chthyologists put the likely figure for bristlemouths at hundreds of trillions – and perhaps quadrillions, or thousands of trillions."

By contrast, the most numerous *land* vertebrate is the chicken, at about 24 billion – thousands, or perhaps millions, of times less than the number of bristlemouths – but still three times more than the number of humans.

Source:
"An Ocean Mystery in the Trillions" by William J. Broad, *NY Times*, June 29, 2015.
https://nyti.ms/2Q4GQxb
Photo: Bristlemouth (Wikimedia Commons – Google Creative Commons)

WONDER 46 -- An Extraordinary Animal: The Tardigrade

Tardigrades are the toughest animals on Earth.

For starters, they look outrageous! Dubbed moss pigs or water bears, tardigrades are very common, microscopic (0.5-1.0 mm) eight-legged animals, with more than 900 species, that have been found in every region of Earth's biosphere. They can: live in temperatures from just above absolute zero to beyond boiling; live under pressures six times greater than the deepest ocean trench and in the vacuum of outer space; survive no food or water for 10 years; be brought back to life after being dried out for 8 years; and survive lethal radiation.

Not all of the tardigrade's capabilities have been explained: the quest for answers is fascinating!

Source:
bbc.com: Jasmin Fox-Skelly (3/13/2015), "Tardigrades return from the dead"
https://bbc.in/3suHdy6
Photo: Tardigrade (insideclimatenews.org)

WONDER 47 -- An Extraordinary Animal: The Mantis Shrimp

A mantis shrimp – possibly the most amazing animal on Earth – sees using five times as many different color receptors as humans have.

Sometimes a single species can inspire jaw-dropping awe. Consider the mantis shrimp, found in tropical and subtropical waters in the Indian and western Pacific Oceans. Dogs have red and green color receptors, allowing them to see blends of those colors. We humans have three – red, green and blue – allowing us to see all the colors of a rainbow (our definition). Butterflies have five color receptors, our three plus two we can't experience, so their rainbow is far broader than ours, containing shades unknown, and unknowable, to us. But the mantis shrimp has . . . *16* color receptors and sees a fantastically multi-hued world that we can't even imagine!

Yet this is only half of its amazing story. It can move its claws at the speed of a rifle bullet, so fast that it boils the water around it and causes a lethal shock wave that can kill its prey even if the strike with the claw misses. Because its claws can hit with enough force to break thick aquarium glass, it is difficult to keep in captivity.

And it's beautiful, to boot. [1] [2]

Sources:
[1] theoatmeal.com: "Why the mantis shrimp is my new favorite animal"   https://bit.ly/32tffrQ
[2] Wikipedia.org: "Mantis shrimp"   https://bit.ly/3ssk6Eb
Photo: Mantis shrimp (Flickr/Klaus Stiefel – Google Creative Commons)

WONDER 48 – Exceptionalism: Genes

We humans do not seem exceptional among animals in terms of our senses and other factors described in the previous several wonders. But perhaps we are exceptional in our genetic makeup, neural networks, or at least our intelligence.

Humans have fewer genes than a grape plant or a water flea.

There are 4,149 genes in an *E.Coli* bacterium; 14,889 in a fruit fly; 16,736 in a chicken; 30,434 in a grape plant; and 31,000 in a Daphnia water flea barely visible to the naked eye. [1]

Humans have 22,333 genes – more than a chicken but less than a grape plant and a water flea. [2]

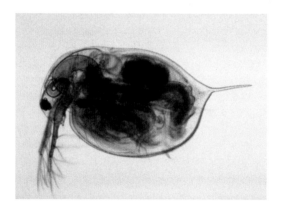

Sources:
[1] EarthSky: "Winner for largest number of genes in any animal known so far. . . a water flea" https://bit.ly/3uY7UwM
[2] ScienceNews: Tina Hesman Saey (10/13/2010), "More than a chicken, fewer than a grape" https://bit.ly/3v49a1c
Photo: Daphnia water flea (Wikimedia Commons – Google Creative Commons)

Humans are 98.4% genetically the same as chimpanzees and 60% the same as fruit flies.

The modern human is 98.4% genetically indistinguishable from the modern chimpanzee. "There is more difference between a zebra and a horse, or between a dolphin and a porpoise, than there is between you and the furry creatures your distant ancestors left behind when they set out to take over the world." [1]

Each human is genetically 99.9% the same as any other human.
A printed version of a human's genetics code would take up 262,000 pages. Of that number, only 500 would be unique to humans.
Mice overlap genetically 85% with humans; cattle 80%; chickens 60%; bananas 60% (!). [2]

"Of all the genes in the human genome, 55 percent were already present in the first animal." [3]

Researchers in Germany and Switzerland "took the gene that controlled the development of a mouse's eye and inserted it into the larva of a fruit fly . . . . [T]he mouse-eye gene not only made a viable eye in the fruit fly, it made a *fly's* eye. Here are two creatures that hadn't shared a common ancestor for 500 million years, yet could swap genetic material as if they were sisters . . . . They found that they could insert *human* DNA into certain cells of flies and the flies would accept it as if it were their own. Over 60 per cent of human genes, it turns out, are fundamentally the same as those found in fruit flies." [4]

Sources:
[1] *A Short History* . . ., p. 452.
[2] Insider: Lydia Ramsey Pflanzer & Samantha Lee (4/3/2018), "Our DNA is 99.9% the same as the person next to us – and we're surprisingly similar to a lot of other living things" https://bit.ly/3tvtdp8
[3] New York Times: Carl Zimmer (5/4/2018), "The Very First Animal Appeared Amid an Explosion of DNA" https://nyti.ms/3srt5Wh
[4] *A Short History* . . ., p. 411.
Photo: Queensland fruit fly (Pixabay – Google Creative Commons)

WONDER 49 – Exceptionalism: Number of Chromosomes

We humans have fewer chromosomes than great white sharks.

Humans have 46 chromosomes in each cell; the Zika mosquito has 6, slime molds have 12, dolphins have 44, chimpanzees have 48, goats have 60, dogs have 78, great white sharks have 82, carp have 104, and the Agrodiaetus butterfly has 268.

Source:
wikipedia.org: "List of organisms by chromosome count"   https://bit.ly/3akKgmn
Photo: Agrodiaetus butterfly (Flickr – Google Creative Commons)

WONDER 50 – Exceptionalism: Number of Neurons

Pound for pound, humans have the most.

An elephant has 267 billion neurons (nerve cells), whereas a human has only 86 billion. However, elephants are tens of times larger (heavier) than humans. Here are the numbers of neurons in some other animals: cat, 760 million; octopus, 500 million; brown rat, 200 million; cockroach, 1 million; ant, 250 thousand; jellyfish, 5,600; sponge, 0. [1]

If all the neurons in a human were lined up end-to-end, they would stretch 600 miles (something to think about when walking a mile). Each neuron is between .004 mm-0.1 mm wide and a fraction of an inch to several feet long. [2]

"Each neuron connects with thousands of other neurons, giving trillions and trillions of connections – as many connections 'in a single cubic centimeter of brain tissue as there are stars in the Milky Way.' " [3]

"Just sitting quietly, doing nothing at all, your brain churns through more information in thirty seconds than the Hubble Space Telescope has processed in thirty years. A morsel of cortex one cubic millimeter in size – about the size of a grain of sand – could hold two thousand terabytes [one terabyte = one trillion bytes] of information, enough to store all the movies ever made, trailers included . . . . Altogether, the human brain is estimated to hold something on the order of two hundred exabytes [one exabyte = 10^{18} or one billion billion bytes] of information, roughly equal to 'the entire digital content of today's world', according to *Nature Neuroscience*." [4]

Sources:

[1] wikipedia.org: "List of animals by number of neurons"   https://bit.ly/3suFFUO
[2] The Guardian: James Randerson (2/28/2012), "How many neurons make a human brain?
Billions fewer than we thought"   https://bit.ly/3ttMgQM
enchantedlearning.com: "The Brain: Brain Cells"   https://bit.ly/3tvG4Ys
[3] *The Body*, p. 50.
[4] *The Body*, p. 49.
Photo: African elephant (Wikimedia Commons – Google Creative Commons)

WONDER 51 – Exceptionalism: Brain Size and Intelligence

How do humans stack up against other animals in terms of brain size and measures of intelligence? (Of course, it is important to remember that intelligence is a human construct to begin with.)

Which animals have the largest brains – and how do you measure that?

It stands to reason that the largest mammals have the largest and heaviest brains. The brain of a sperm whale weighs 18 pounds (8.1 kg); an elephant, 11 pounds (5.0 kg); and a dolphin, 3.5 pounds (1.6 kg). These are all animals heavier than humans. Our brains weigh about 3.1 pounds (1.4 kg).

Source:
wikipedia.org: "Brain size"   https://bit.ly/2Qvc28x

Which animals have the largest brains for their size?

What is the ratio of an animal's brain to its body mass?
For humans of average size, that ratio is 1:50. For many animals we are familiar with, that ratio is much smaller. For an elephant, praised for its intelligence, the brain is only 1/560 of its body mass. For a shark the ratio is 1:2,496 and for a hippopotamus, it is 1:2,789. Cats and dogs have brain-to-body mass ratios of 1:110 and 1:125, respectively. However, some smaller animals have much larger brains relative to their size than humans do: mouse, 1:40; small bird, 1:14, tree shrew, 1:10; and an ant, whose intelligence we admire in the aggregate, a remarkable 1:7!

Source:
wikipedia.org: "Brain to body-mass ratio"   https://bit.ly/32sNFeh
Photos: Sperm whale (Wikimedia Commons – Google Creative Commons); Carpenter ant (PxHere – Google Creative Commons)

In gauging intelligence, scientists have developed the concept of "encephalization quotient"; that is, the ratio between the actual brain size and the *predicted* brain size for an animal of a given size. Does an animal have a larger or smaller brain than you would expect, given its body size? An animal with a brain of just the size you would expect would have an encephalization quotient of 1.0. Here are some encephalization quotients for familiar non-human animals: horse, 0.9; cat, 1.0; dog 1.2; elephant, 1.75; chimpanzee, 2.65; dolphin, 4.14. This does look like a scale of intelligence, at least as we humans think of the concept. What about humans, what is their encephalization quotient? 7.6! This is the highest encephalization ratio among mammals. [1]

Here is an interesting observation on human brain size, over time. You may have heard that Neanderthal brains were larger than those of modern *Homo sapiens.*

In fact, our brains "are much smaller today than they were ten thousand or twelve thousand years ago, and by quite a lot. The average brain has shrunk from 1,500 cubic centimeters then to 1,350 cubic centimeters now. That's equivalent to scooping out a portion of the brain about the size of a tennis ball." [2]

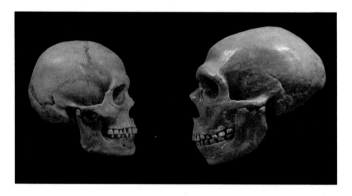

Sources:
[1] Wikipedia.org: "Encephalization quotient"   https://bit.ly/3tuY31h
[2] *The Body*, p. 70.
Photo: *Homo sapiens* and Neanderthal skulls (Wikimedia Commons – Google Creative Commons)

WONDER 52 – Who Will Be Here After We're Gone?

As the curtain descends on this book, it's only fitting that we contemplate what happens when humans leave the earthly stage. Which animals are most likely to adapt to whatever changes or new conditions cause our demise?

Rats are ideally suited to take over if humans disappear from Earth.

It may not be as noble a trait as intelligence, which we humans value most highly, but longevity – the ability to endure as a species – certainly merits wonder, maybe even awe. According to paleobiologist Jan Zalasiewicz, the species most likely to survive after we humans are gone are the super-adapters, able to adjust to climate changes and who knows what other stressors. These include cockroaches, crows and snakes, but chief among them are rats. [1]

Bacteria were on Earth billions of years before us and will be on Earth long after us.

"Bacteria may not build cities or have interesting social lives, but they will be here when the Sun explodes. This is their planet, and we are on it only because they allow us to be. Bacteria, never forget, got along for billions of years without us. We couldn't survive a day without them." [2]

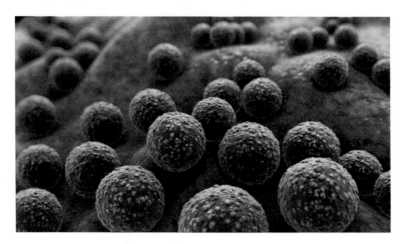

Sources:
[1] npr.org: Flora Lichtman (9/24/2015),"A World Without Humans Looks a Lot Like a Rat Race"
https://n.pr/2RAoUdZ
Zalasiewicz, Jan. *The Earth After Us.* 2009, OUP: Oxford.
[2] *A Short History. . .*, p. 303.
Photos: Brown rat (Wikimedia Commons – Google Creative Commons); Staphylococcus bacteria
(Wikimedia Commons – Google Creative Commons)

WONDERS AND WONDERMENT –
AND RELIGION

What is the purpose of religion? Why have religions developed and proliferated over the last five thousand years? Sociologist Emile Durkheim saw three functions of religion in human society, three reasons for their existence:
1) a promotion of social cohesion, drawing people together through shared beliefs and rituals;
2) a means of social control in the form of sets of morals and rules for good behavior;
3) a source of answers to existential questions such as how we humans got here, how the world works and what forces control the natural world.
All societies have some form of religion that fulfills these functions to varying degrees. [1]

How do the wonders and corresponding wonderment in this book relate to these functions of religion? Any relation to the first two functions – social cohesion and social control – is not obvious: more about that later. However, the wonders do help us situate ourselves in the world by illuminating the dimensions in which we exist. We gain a better picture of how we are situated in the cosmos, of our relative size and importance, of our "specialness" vis-à-vis the specialness of other life. They help us "find ourselves" as humans, help us know where and who we are.

The world's major religions in terms of numbers – Christianity and Islam – offer non-scientific answers to existential questions. This is not surprising: how could it be any other way given their age, both coming into being almost a thousand years before the advancements and spread of scientific knowledge in the Renaissance? Back then, Earth was at the center of a known universe almost infinitely smaller than the one we know about today. Dimensions and the scale of things were determined by the naked eye, by personal experience and by credence in tales of others. The apex position of man among animals was assumed because so little was known of other species. Creation myths (for man and for the universe) and powerful, unknowable deities filled in for scientific explanations to satisfy people's need for answers. And answers were needed, because the alternatives were ignorance and fear. Before the Big Bang and evolution, before the principles of our modern sciences, Genesis and other Biblical (or Quranic) stories had to suffice.

Today we have – if we are willing to look – scientific explanations for previously mystifying phenomena. These explanations are based on provable principles, not on mythology. Such knowledge should serve to dispel fear as it replaces ignorance. It may even bring a sense of calm and peace. It may even be religion.

The wonders in this book are not miracles: quite the opposite, they are the results of scientific investigation. They are real. Although they may stretch our credulity, they do not depend on magic or suspending one's belief in physical and natural laws.

What of wonderment in relation to religion? Are wonder and awe important to Christianity and Islam? Certainly. It is vital to the acceptance of powerful myths that try to explain the world that they are regarded as awesome. Religions can inspire wonder and wonderment, often in the form of miracles, events or phenomena not explicable by natural or scientific laws. "According to a 2011 poll by the Pew Research Center, more than 90 percent of evangelical Christians believe miracles still take place." [2] By contrast, the wonders in this book are grounded in science, in demonstrable explanations. Questions are truly answered even as more questions are generated, as is the way of scientific inquiry. The wonderment inspired is pure, suffused with awe and lacking in fear. Contemplation of the wonders brings admiration, respect, even joy.

Knowledge is powerful. Knowing the answers can give us a feeling of pride in accomplishment. It may inflate our sense of superiority as a species. And yet, if anything, the wonders in this book instill humility. We are in awe of the new dimensions of the world we inhabit that are revealed, but we are also humbled. Discovering the immensity of the universe shrinks our individual importance. Understanding evolution lets us see how lucky we are as a species. Learning about the tininess of atoms and the incredible multitudes of microscopic life makes us realize that a lot more is going on in the world than we thought, beyond our formerly limited scope. Uncovering the amazing abilities of other animals situates us anew, not at the apex, but as one among many living things.

Let's look back to Durkheim's first function of religion, providing social cohesion. Research has shown that such cohesion through religion may increase happiness and reduce stress. Contemplation of wonders may reasonably also have these effects, although there are no studies to show it. Group acceptance of the wonders can promote social cohesion, but even on an individual level there are benefits. Personally, I am very happy with my expanded knowledge of a greater world. It even gives me a sort of contentment, that I have penetrated some of the mystery of the world's dimensions and workings. And a state of personal contentment surely aids social cohesion.

One unfortunate possible outcome of religious adherence is religious fanaticism. As has been all too evident throughout history, and has been pointed out by atheists, overheated religious adherence can lead to hatred, violence, wars, deaths. The belief that "My god is better than your god" has ignited horrendous conflicts between and among religions that profess peace and love. Many religions worship a deity, either a real person or a human-like creation. Many have human prophets who interpret or disseminate their god's words. Most are focused on people. And people are fallible.

What about contemplation of wonders in relation to that pitfall of religions, violence? Would a religion focused not on people and their works but on the natural world and its wonders be less likely to divide people against one another? It seems reasonable, perhaps likely. None of the wonders described in this book are the works of man. They are pure scientific truth. Reaction to these wonders does not depend on worshipping any particular human beings or siding with any particular groups of people. The wonders are part of the natural world of **all** people, and equally so. Each of us may feel the same wonderment before these revelations. My wonders are the same as yours; we have no need to fight over them; they do not divide us as conventional religious beliefs do. Appreciation of nature's wonders is unifying: my wonders are no better or worse than yours because they are the same for all of us. Before these wonders, as before all of the natural world, we stand arm in arm, humbly, in peaceful appreciation. Furthermore, contemplation of wonders and the resulting wonderment are not sexist: there is no domination of male gods and prophets among the living and non-living stuff of the natural world.

Not only does a wonders-based religion have a different relationship to people than traditional religions, but it has a different relationship to time. The world's religions have starting points, often beginning with the birth of a person who spread new ideas. Did Christianity and Islam exist before Jesus and Mohammed? Did God/Allah? There is no starting point for wonders. Some have existed essentially forever. Others have appeared as the universe has changed and the stream of evolution has flowed over billions of years. Their existence is independent of man. Before anyone was aware of these wonders, they existed. As a basis of religion, as objects of wonderment, their existence has largely been *revealed* through science. There is no human author of these wonders, no book that enumerates them (*this* book is merely a sampler), and most pre-date humans.

Finally, Durkheim posits that religions are important for social control, for sets of morals and prescriptions of behaviors that will help all get along harmoniously. Religions not only bind communities but when faithfully adhered to, assure the good of all. Unfortunately, the prescriptions and proscriptions of religions differ one from another, thereby providing another source of division and conflict. Not only is my *god* better than yours, but so are my *rules*.

117

Can wonders and wonderment help us live better, more just and righteous lives? Isn't this the ultimate test of a religion? By promoting humility before awesome common knowledge shared by all, they may reduce a desire for conflict. The admiration and respect devolving from wonderment are directed at the wonderful world of us all, a uniting rather than dividing force. The focus is on the marvels of the natural world that we all share, not on the various laws of diverse tribes. We all see and revere the same beautiful sunset, as it were.

However, likely more is needed in order for contemplation of wonders to satisfactorily guide our lives. That missing element could be the one egalitarian moral principle that virtually all religions share, the Golden Rule: Do unto others as you would have them do unto you. The wording may be different in different faiths, but the meaning is the same.

So finally, is the amazingness of the world as revealed by science and demonstrated by the wonders in this book a sufficient basis for a religion? For the reasons cited above, I humbly assert that the quiet contemplation of the wonders of the natural world that leads to wonderment, *plus* adherence to the Golden Rule, is religion enough in our modern world.

[Note: I have restricted my writing about religion here to Christianity and Islam, deity-based faiths I am familiar with. I have enough knowledge of Judaism to include it with those two, as well. However, I am not familiar enough with other major world religions, such as Hinduism and Buddhism, to confidently generalize my statements to them. And, of course, there are myriad other faiths across a broad spectrum that I do not address. Nevertheless, I am confident that my conclusions about the validity and value of contemplation of wonders and experiencing wonderment are not diminished by these omissions.]

Sources for "Wonders and Wonderment and Religion":
https://courses.lumenlearning.com/boundless-sociology/chapter/the-functionalist-perspective-on-religion
[1] Durkheim, Emile (1912). *Les formes élémentaires de la vie religieuse (The Elementary Forms of Religious Life)*. Translated by Joseph Swain. London: George Allen & Unwin, Ltd.
[2] Wikipedia,"Miracle"

APOLOGIA

My maternal great-grandfather was the politician and orator – and religious fundamentalist – William Jennings Bryan. Growing up, I was proud of his accomplishments – three-time Democratic candidate for President, Secretary of State under President Woodrow Wilson, leader of the Democratic Party for a generation, deliverer of the "Cross of Gold" speech, champion of women's rights and workers' rights – but I was embarrassed by the ridicule he received as the defender of creationism at the infamous Scopes Monkey Trial. Watching his portrayal in the film "Inherit the Wind" was particularly painful.

My mother and her father (William Jennings Bryan's son and my beloved grandfather) felt the sting of public derision to such an extent that they both spurned organized religion and were atheists. I grew up with a suspicion of religion, uneasy about the harm that it could inflict on one's well-being. I saw religions as divisive, us-versus-them propositions. If not downright harmful, they were at least, in my view, unnecessary.

It is against this backdrop that I see the wonders of nature as revealed by science, and the sense of wonderment that they engender, as valid substitutes for all organized religions. Combined with a strong belief in the Golden Rule, they are, I believe, sufficient to guide each of us toward leading a full and good life.

Thank you, reader, for reading (and hopefully enjoying) this book.

"Why these blank pages at the end of this book?"

They are here for you to use for reflections on the wonders and other parts of the book. And they are a place where you may write down *other* wonders that have influenced your life.

Author's Biosketch

Al Forsyth is a retired professor of Teacher Education (Weber State University, Ogden, UT). Born in commuter-belt New York, he attended Brown University (B.A., French Literature, 1967), Columbia University (M.A., Geography, 1972) and Utah State University (Ed.D., Educational Technology, 1987).
Before his career in higher education, he worked at Battelle Memorial Institute in Columbus, OH, as an educational writer, and at the National Geographic Society in Washington, DC, as an educational materials designer.

Al and his wife are "empty nesters", living in Logan, UT, and "snow-birding" in Tucson, AZ. They have two married children and three grandchildren who are just starting to experience the wonders of the world. Al enjoys hiking, golfing (required by his Scottish ancestry) and playing the cello. He is currently between dogs.

His favorite saying is "Moderation in all things, including moderation."

Made in the USA
Las Vegas, NV
12 December 2021

37292734R00074